101 *More* Ways to Make **Training** *Active*

Elaine Biech

WILEY

Library of Congress Cataloging-in-Publication Data is on file.

9781118971956 (pbk)

9781118971970 (ePDF)

9781118971963 (epub)

Printed in the United States of America

10 9 8 7 6 5 4 3 2 1

CONTENTS

OPEN EVERY SESSION ACTIVELY   41

Icebreakers and Introductions   43

Identifying Participant Expectations   56

DELIVERING ACTIVE LEARNING   73

Connecting Learning to the Workplace   75

Engaging Participants in Learning   81

For free Active Training tips and tools, please visit www.wiley.com/go/activetraining and use the password **professional.**

ACKNOWLEDGMENTS

This book would not be in your hands without the resourceful people who took time to share 101 of their most creative ideas. Thank you to all contributors. Sharing your best inspires me and will motivate readers to incorporate your activities into their learning sessions. I am pleased to publish your name on your contribution's page.

An extra special thank you goes out to the Above and Beyond Band of Achievers (ABBA) who tweeted, texted, and called their colleagues; contributed extra activities; volunteered to help; and were involved in 101 other ways: Wendy Axelrod, Peter Garber, Barbara Glacel, Karen Lawson, Lynne Lazaroff, Dawn Mahoney, Renie McClay, Kella Price, Kimberly Seeger, Tracy Tagliati, Shannon Tipton, and Amy Tolbert. I appreciate your extra help to make this volume excellent.

The Wiley people who are behind the scenes but up front with expertise include Matt Davis for reviving the series and production editor Chaitanya Mella.

INTRODUCTION:
GETTING THE MOST
FROM THIS RESOURCE

You can tell people what they need to know very fast.
But they will forget what you tell them even faster.
People are more likely to understand what they figure out
for themselves than what you figure out for them.

—Mel Silberman

It's been 10 years since Mel Silberman's second edition of *101 Ways to Make Training Active*, and exactly 20 years since the first edition. So it is fitting that 2015 has been selected for the third edition.

Mel's staunch advocates are still following his active learning concepts and contributing to the profession to ensure that participants have the opportunity to figure things out for themselves and transfer their knowledge and skills back to the workplace.

Mel's unwavering support is based on the fact that his concepts work. Training is "active" when the learners do most of the work. Learners consider the content, solve problems, make decisions, and practice the skills. This ensures that they are ready to apply what they learned once they return to the workplace or wherever they intend to use their newly acquired skills and knowledge.

What's new? All of the activities are new. Unlike editions one and two where many of the tried and true activities and tips were the same, everything in edition three is new. We've tapped the experts in the field to help. Due to the unwavering support of

Mel's concepts by a legion of followers, we have invited others to contribute to this book and join in sharing how they make training active. Facilitators, coaches, designers, e-learning experts, trainers, and others responded and contributed their techniques to this book. Many have come full circle, giving Mel's concepts and ideas credit for the spinoff idea. You will find their names associated with their contributions.

What is "active" training? You can tell you are in an "active" classroom because participants are out of their seats, moving about, sharing ideas, and totally involved—both mentally and physically. Active training is fast-paced, fun, and personally engaging for learners. *101 Ways to Make Training Active* contains specific, practical techniques that can be used for almost any topic area. The activities are designed to enliven, engage, and ensure that learners are involved in their own learning.

When well-developed, a live-classroom environment has the ability to motivate learners in special ways, including a personal engagement with a caring facilitator, the social recognition and reinforcement of the learner's peers, and the dramatic presentation of content. Yet, most of us no longer rely on only classroom delivery, so the online learning that we all deliver also needs to be active. With a bit of tweaking, other formats can be equally enhanced with the techniques in this book.

Although this collection is based on learning in a classroom, many of the activities and tips also work in an online setting. In some cases the contributor shares that information. Because classroom delivery is not the only option, a second companion resource, *101 Ways to Make Learning Beyond the Classroom Active*, focuses on alternative learning events that occur outside a classroom setting: coaching, online, informal, and others.

How This Book Is Organized

Top Ten Lists

The contents begin with Mel's famous "Top Ten Lists." Like edition one and two, this edition features 200+ all new tips. We are excited that Karen Lawson, who worked on the first two editions, was willing to go back in time to reminisce about Mel's favorite tips. It's a great way to start this section. The rest of the list is arranged to some degree in the order that you, as a facilitator, might use these tips starting with 10 tips to open an active learning session to 10 options to close an active learning session. Between you will find 10 tips to become an engaging facilitator, 10 storytelling tips, 10 strategies for forming groups, and 10 ways to address challenging situations. You will also find these lists on the matching website so that you will be able to download them and keep them within easy reach while you are designing or while you are in front of a classroom.

101 Ways

The 101 techniques described in this book are divided into five sections. Each is described here to help you know where to find the technique that will be most beneficial. Again, the techniques are arranged to some degree in the order that you, as a facilitator, might use the techniques.

Open Every Session Actively

This section contains icebreakers, introduction techniques, ways to identify participant needs, and other kinds of opening activities. These activities provide you with techniques to start your learning sessions off right—with participants taking an active role right from the start.

- Icebreakers and Introductions: introduces participants to each other and the content; reveals participant expertise and experiences with the content; offers opportunities for participant to be involved and speak early.
- Identifying Participant Expectations: facilitates cooperation and understanding of participant attitudes and current level of skills and knowledge; helps to clarify what will and will not happen in the session; tips off facilitator about the potential need to adjust the delivery plan.

Delivering Active Learning

This section contains techniques that can be used throughout a learning session. The activities remind you of the critical elements to keep learning active: how to get participants involved, tie the content to the real world, allow for practice, and encourage participants to share what they know with their peers.

- Connecting Learning to the Workplace: ensures that throughout the learning session you have ways to remind learners that it's all about what they take back to the workplace that counts.

- Engaging Participants in Learning: reminds us that engagement equals learning and that using unique techniques is a great way to garner engagement.

- Enhance Learning with Practice: acknowledges that practice is the best way to enable learning, especially when you are able to set up the classroom with practical situations that learners will face upon their return to the workplace.

- Learn with Your Peers: recognizes the value that all learners bring to the classroom based on their expertise and experience; helps participants sort out what they understand, what they still need to learn, and what questions they may have as they lead their own learning.

Content to Support Active Learning

This section presents specific content for the most common topics delivered: communication, diversity, leadership, and teamwork. The content works well as a part of a session with the same title or built into another type of learning session. For example the communication activities could be a part of a managerial skills session as new managers learn the import part that communication plays in their role as a manager.

- Communication: offers content ideas and twists to the one skill that most of us still need to work on; introduces the importance of stories and words in communication; expands awareness of generational differences and challenges we all face.

- Diversity and Inclusion: provides new ideas and activities for a topic our organizations continue to struggle with.

- Leadership: suggests ideas to develop skills for leaders at all levels; addresses a topic plaguing most organizations with a shortage of prepared leaders for the future; offers a mix of skills and reflection.

- Teamwork and Team Building: provides a nice mix of skill development, knowledge of teamwork, and building a team when things are not working as well as they should.

Tools to Facilitate Active Learning

This section offers an assortment of tools that can be used in almost any area and with any content: energizers when energy is lagging, experiential learning to allow participants to experience the learning, feedback to give and receive advice and opinions, ideas to stimulate discussion, and tips for the logistics of juggling a successful classroom.

- Energizers: ideas to keep learners active and participating, even during the afternoon doldrums with unique ideas you won't find anywhere else.

- Experiential Learning: develops your repertoire of methods to give learners opportunities to experience the learning; easy to adapt to any topic and still maintain the format.

- Feedback: offers means to build learners' skill by receiving recommendations and advice to improve in a safe environment.

- Manage a Classroom: addresses challenges of every sort including moving participants into groups, bringing participants back on time, addressing difficult participants and situations, and facilitating an environment that considers learners' needs.

- Stimulate Discussion: introduces ideas to encourage dialogue and conversation to help participants sort through what is meaningful to them and what to implement upon the return to their workplace.

Closing and Follow-Up for Active Learning

This section goes beyond the classroom. It ensures that you have ideas and tools to conclude a learning session so that participants reflect and review what they have learned and how they can apply it back on the job. Numerous ways to practice, analyze, and internalize the content are presented.

- Application: delivers creative ways to help learners determine how they will apply the knowledge and skills from the session; offers support and planning for the return to the real world and challenges them to think through the possibilities.

- Closing Practice and Review: offers one last time for learners to review what they learned or practice skills before returning to the workplace; offers approaches that work for various types of employees.

- Closing Summaries and Evaluation: presents ideas for how to bring it all together and to prioritize critical facts and ideas; ensures that themes are clarified and feedback is offered about the session.

- Transfer Learning Actions: transfers support after the session is over through groups, pairs, and other ways to keep the learning alive; ensures that what was learned is not "shelved" for implementation at another time, but applied immediately.

Activity Design

Each of the 101 strategies is arranged in a similar format, making it easy for you to go directly to the element that you need. Six elements describe each of the 101 activities:

Overview: a statement about the purpose of the strategy and the setting and situation in which it is appropriate.

Participants: number of participants that the author suggests is appropriate for the strategy and in some cases a definition of the type or level of employee that is required.

Procedure: step-by-step instructions about how to use the strategy and things to remember to make it successful.

Debrief: suggested questions or actions you can use to bring the activity to a close. This may be the most important part of the activity. The debriefing should ensure that participants understand the content and are able to transfer it to the workplace.

Variations: suggested alternatives for ways to use the strategy.

Case Examples: situations in which the strategy has been used to help you visualize how it can be implemented.

Whether you use the 10 Tips lists or the 101 strategies, they serve to build a range of "active learning" methods and offer tools to design the best active learning sessions possible.

200 Tips to Make Training Active and Learning Successful

Two Hundred Tips

Active Training for successful learning requires you to be aware of myriad details. In true Mel Silberman–style, I've continued his tradition by opening this book with two hundred tips that address many of these details. The tips cover everything from opening to closing a classroom session and include introductions, storytelling tips, and presentation tactics. You'll find ideas for becoming an engaged facilitator, keeping your learners focused, and addressing challenging situations.

The top 10 lists in this chapter, 20 of them with over 200 training tips, summarize best practices and ideas for how to address some of the issues and challenges that you face. We are fortunate to have tapped into some of the best trainers in the world for these tips to make your life easier.

You have probably heard of some of these tips and already used many. Mel believed that having organized lists of ideas in one place makes your job easier. Someone recently described these top 10 lists as a "bonus" to trainers. I agree. The organized lists provide ideas in a flash for some of the questions you have most often.

To celebrate Mel and what he has done for our profession, I asked Karen Lawson to create the first list: "Mel's Top 10 Training Tips." Karen worked closely with Mel on the first and second edition of this book. This list of the best-of-the-best tips will give you pause to think about your own training style and how well you implement each of these tips.

Top 10 Lists

1. Mel's Top 10 Training Tips
2. 10 Tips to Open a Learning Session Actively
3. 10 Tactics for Relevant Icebreakers

1 | Mel's Top 10 Training Tips

Mel Silberman was the originator of the "Top 10 Training Tips" in his *101 Ways to Make Training Active* books. It is fitting that we honor him by beginning this set of top 10 by remembering his personal top 10:

1. **It's not what you give them; it's what they take away that counts.** Our minds are like sponges as we soak up knowledge and information. When sponges are saturated, any additional water will run right through. Just as the sponge is overloaded, a learner can experience cognitive overload when he or she receives more information than the brain can store in its working memory. It doesn't matter how much information you disseminate. If the learner does not retain that information, learning has not taken place. The challenge to the trainer is to present information in such a way that participants do not experience overload.

2. **You can't hide in a pair.** Don't overlook the power of pairs to promote active learning. Asking participants to work with learning partners is an efficient and effective active-learning technique. It guarantees 100 percent participation.

3. **Telling is not training.** The belief that "I gave them the information," "covered the material," or "told them how to do it" is very misleading for both the trainer and the learner. Telling, explaining, or lecturing does not guarantee the receiver of the information understands it. Learning is not an automatic result of pouring information into another person's head. People learn by doing, not by being told.

4. **Distinguish between "need-to-know" and "nice-to-know."** When designing your training program, focus on what participants absolutely need to know. This is particularly important when there are time constraints. Don't try to cram eight hours of content into a two-hour program. By clearly defining objectives for what participants will know and be able to do by the end of the sessions, trainers clarify content and select appropriate learning strategies.

5. **Inquiring minds want to know.** Human beings are naturally curious. If you have any doubt, just watch young children exploring and learning about the world around them. Take advantage of that innate curiosity. Create learning

---

Contributed by Karen Lawson, Lawson Consulting Group, Inc.

experiences that require the learner to seek something such as an answer to a question, information to solve a problem, or ways to do his or her job.

6. **When training is active, the participants do the work.**   Participants work in concert, encouraging and facilitating one another's efforts to achieve, complete tasks, and reach the group's goals. People understand concepts better and retain information longer when they are actively involved with the learning process. The trainer's role is to create an environment in which learning takes place and to facilitate the learning process.

7. **People will remember what they figure out for themselves.**   One of a trainer's objectives is to get participants to think. Learning experiences that require participants to use their minds will result in better retention, both long term and short term.

8. **Get them active from the start.**   Getting people involved from the very beginning through some type of opening activity accomplishes several purposes. Techniques that immediately involve participants are very effective in piquing interest, arousing curiosity, and preparing them for the learning experience. They can help reduce tension and anxieties, energize the group, set a tone for the session, and involve everyone. Most importantly, opening activities communicate to the participants that they are not going to sit back and be passive learners or receivers of information.

9. **It's not about you.**   Focus on your audience, not on yourself. Unfortunately, some trainers are more concerned about showcasing themselves and demonstrating how much they know. When you put the needs of the learner first, you automatically change the way you design and deliver training.

10. **When I *hear*, I forget. When I *hear* and *see*, I remember a little. When I *hear*, *see*, and *ask questions* or *discuss* with someone else, I begin to understand. When I *hear*, *see*, *discuss*, and *do*, I acquire knowledge and skill. When I *teach* to another, I master.**   This Active Learning Credo is a modification of what Confucius declared over 2400 years ago: "What I *hear*, I forget. What I *see*, I remember. What I *do*, I understand." It sums up Mel's passion for the profession; however, as Mel did so often, he took a great idea and improved it.

2 | 10 Tips to Open a Learning Session Actively

The opening of your training is critical. You know what they say: "You only have once to make a first impression." Your opening sets the stage for the rest of the training session—whether it is in person in a classroom or online. You will want to accomplish five objectives in your opening: stimulate interest and enthusiasm, understand your participants' needs, initiate active participation, clarify expectations, and help everyone get to know each other. Avoid the usual opening: welcome, name, objectives, emergency information, and ground rules. Yikes! That's a sure bet for an inactive session. These suggestions will help you to accomplish the five objectives for opening an active training session.

Stimulate interest and enthusiasm.
1. Build in an element of surprise by using unusual props or a shocking statement. Use relevant humor, anecdotes, or stories that make a point about the session content.
2. Use a short exercise or demonstration that supports the topic.

Understand your participants' needs.
3. Use questions or small groups to identify content needs. You could pose questions that start with, "How many of you…?" or "What questions did you bring with you today?"
4. Address esteem needs by learning something about participants' experience and expertise that they bring to the learning session. This suggests that you want them to share what they know with others.

Initiate active participation.
5. Get participants up and moving around and interacting with other participants to establish that the session will be interactive and they have a role in their learning. If you are online, ensure that your participants are involved early.
6. Ask a question. Even a polling question that requires a simple raised hand (classroom or e-learning) is an early indicator that you expect active participation. Choose your questions so that most participants can respond affirmatively and raise their hands.

Ideas from Kenneth Stein, EdD, CPLP, SPHR, Successful Endeavors

Clarify expectations.

7. Ask participants to share why they are attending the training and what they are expecting to learn or happen. You could ask for their hopes and fears, what they need to learn to make the day worthwhile, or how well their expectations match the objectives.

8. Equally important is to clarify if participants' expectations go beyond the scope of the training design. Tell them how you will handle this such as meeting with them after the session, adjusting content to accommodate the expectations, providing supplemental material after the session, or other ways.

Help everyone get to know each other.

9. Ensure that you have an icebreaker (see "10 Tactics for Relevant Icebreakers") or plan for introductions (see "10 Participant Introductions") that allow participants to move around and greet others. Everyone should speak at least once during the opening and should hear the name of everyone in the session.

10. In addition to a getting-to-know-you exercise, use table tents. Have participants place their names on both sides during the introductions. This allows you and other participant so see the names from all angles.

3   10 Tactics for Relevant Ice Breakers

An icebreaker is a structured activity usually used at the beginning of a training session to initiate participation and introductions. The key purpose of icebreakers is to help everyone get to know each other, but an icebreaker can accomplish a whole lot more. A well-crafted icebreaker is tied to the program content and outcomes and is relevant to the participants. It is conducted in a relaxed atmosphere with no pressure to "produce" and increases the participants comfort levels. It allows participants to learn a little more about the other participants and gently transitions them into the content. Icebreakers also give you an opportunity to observe the group to learn something about individuals and their interaction with each other.

1. **Bingo.**   Bingo is probably the most used icebreaker and the reason is that it works. Create a bingo card on a sheet of paper. Instead of having B-3 or N-13, each square has information written. It could be very specific, such as "played a saxophone in high school" or general so that it relates to many people, such as "plays a musical instrument." Try to include some questions about the topics, such as "is a new supervisor" if you are facilitating a supervisory skills session. Each person signs only one square per card.

2. **Declarations.**   Divide the audience into small groups. Have each group write one declaration for what they will learn by the end the end of the session. Post the declarations and weave them into the learning experience.

3. **Ask questions.**   This can be done with the entire group or in small groups. Assign a lighthearted question or two but help participants slide into the content such as: "What is it you wish you knew how to do well with regard to [the content]?" "What lessons did Mom (or a favorite teacher) teach you to help you adjust to [this content]?"

4. **Human graphs.**   Ask a series of questions related to the content such as, "How many of you need today's content to do a better job?" Instead of having people raise their hands in response, have them stand up. Ask participants to report the survey results in percentages, for example, 80 percent of the audience stood as affirmation of the statement.

Ideas from Marcia Stokes, Ogletree Deakins Law Firm

5. **Go to your corners.**   Post four flipchart pages (or online use four chat rooms) that generate some curiosity, such as travel, reading, running, and gourmet cooking. Ask participants to select one and move to that part of the room. Once there, they introduce themselves to the others and tell why they selected the corner they did. After a few minutes they will look on the other side of the flipchart to find a content-related question to address as a small group and report back to the larger group. This can lead directly into the first content module.

6. **Spell it.**   Participants take one letter from the course title and use it to explain what they hope to learn. For example, in a Change Management class, someone could say, "I selected 'C' for 'communication,' because I want to know how and when to communicate change better."

7. **Picture me.**   Have crayons scattered around the table. Ask participants to decorate their table tent to better define their goal for the session. They can introduce themselves and their goals in pairs or trios before introducing themselves to the entire group.

8. **My boss expects.**   Form small groups and have them identify what their bosses expect them to learn in the session and bring back to the workplace.

9. **Trainer for a minute.**   Invite pairs to imagine they are teaching this class. Have each pair identify what one thing would they be sure to include. Allow 90 seconds for introductions and topic discussion. Then have them mix again and pair with another person. Do this as many times as you have time allowed. Facilitate a discussion that leads into the objectives of the session.

10. **Autographs.**   This activity requires that you create a handout that lists 15 to 25 questions or statements that can be "autographed" by participants who match the description. Include some personal statements such as "Has been to Asia." Content-related statements will help you ease into the session. A communications training session may include statements such as "Have been told I am a good listener" or "Spends at least 59 percent of my time on the job communicating."

4 10 Participant Introductions

Literally hundreds of ways exist for you to conduct introductions. So why would any-one start at one end of the group and go around in a circle? There is no reason. Enjoy experimenting with this part of your training. You'll have just as much fun as your participants.

1. **Introduce you.** It is sometimes easier to introduce others than to introduce yourself. Participants pair up and learn something that can be shared with the rest of the group, including an interesting thought about the content.

2. **Creative questions.** Provide a list of questions and ask participants to introduce themselves by answering one question. Here are examples: "If your life was a TV program or movie, what would it be called?" "What is your favorite word and can you connect it to this course?" "What famous person are you most like?"

3. **Two truths and a lie.** Participants make three statements about themselves: Two are true and one is false. The other participants try to guess the false statement.

4. **Little-known fact.** Share something that no one knows or would guess about you.

5. **Mingle.** Ask everyone to move around and introduce themselves to others. Ask them to identify something they have in common with others and something that is different from others.

6. **Double the pairs.** Assign each participant another's name. They could draw them out of a hat. Have them locate one another and introduce themselves. Ask the pairs to combine with another pair, and all four introduce each other. If you have a large group, you could have each quad combine with another quad for a final round of introductions.

7. **Roll of the dice.** Create six questions and assign each a number from one to six. Each person rolls the dice and answers the corresponding question. If you have table groups or a particularly large group, you could complete the introductions in small groups.

Ideas from Marlene Caroselli, Center for Professional Development and Dr. Kella Price, SPHR, CPLP, Price Consulting Group

  8. Share successes.   Have participants start the session in a celebratory mood. Have
  them introduce themselves and add, "This week I am excited because I…"

  9. What's your bag?   Have participants draw a picture and add a slogan to a brown
  paper bag that answers the questions, "What's your bag? Who are you?" In a team
  building session, you could have them hang the bags on the wall and ask team
  members to add comments to the bags.

  10. Tweet intros.   If you have little time or the session is short, ask participants
  to tweet their introduction in 140 characters. The introduction would include
  their name, department, or company name, plus 144 characters of interest to the
  group. Allow a few minutes for participants to write their tweets.

5   10 Tips to Create an Enticing Learning Environment

Creating a comfortable and enticing learning environment sets the mood for participants to be more receptive to learning. These techniques spark curiosity and create intrigue so the learners want to discover more. Creating a theme takes time, forethought, and preparation, but the result is well worth it.

1. **Use bright colors.**   Bright colors excite the mind. Use colored paper for handouts, colored 3″ × 5″ cards for activities, and brightly colored pipe cleaners or fidget toys on the tables.

2. **Use creative titles and themes for the topic.**   Instead of "Using PowerPoint Effectively" try "Avoiding PowerPoint Pitfalls" and give your presentation an adventurers theme. Instead of "Conflict Management" try "Working with Wild Beasts" and give the presentation a safari theme. Instead of "Customer Service" try "Earn Yourself a Five Star Rating," give the presentation a restaurant or hotel theme.

3. **Play dress up.**   Using the previous examples wear khaki, a pith helmet, and some binoculars around your neck; dress up like a lion tamer or circus leader; or dress up as a waiter or waitress and escort the learners to their seats as they arrive.

4. **Use decorations that inspire curiosity.**   Using the previous examples, try safari themed decorations, or hang posters of inspirational quotes.

5. **Inspirational quotes.**   Find relevant inspirational quotes about your topic. Use PowerPoint templates to make them colorful and visually enticing. Print and tape them around the training room. For leadership development you might use Zig Ziglar's quote: "People often say that motivation doesn't last. Well, neither does bathing; that's why we recommend it daily." For customer service you might borrow from Lewis Carroll: "One of the deep secrets of life is that all that is really worth doing is what we do for others."

6. **Use a theme song.**   Pick a song that matches the theme of your training. Play it as participants arrive, on breaks, and in celebration at the end of the class. The learners can also discuss why the song is relevant to the class or have them

Ideas from Rachel Stromberg, Mad Cowford Improv

pick a song that they think is relevant. Be sure to follow appropriate copyright usage practices.

7. **Use props.** For product training or new hire orientation, have some of the products your organization produces on the tables. For supervisory skills collect a variety of hats to discuss the "many hats a supervisor wears." Get creative and economical by using items from a dollar store. Be sure there is a logical link between the topic and the prop you are using.

8. **Provide incentives.** Adults enjoy prizes and incentives. Your organization may have marketing tchotchkes or small recognition gifts you can use, or you can check out local discount stores for inexpensive items that support a theme. Make it even more special and relate the incentives to the training.

9. **Use intriguing transitions.** Build curiosity as you transition from one topic to the next by using a statement or asking a question that excites the learners to want to know more. For example in a communication session ask, "Have you ever wanted your employees, spouse, or teenager to *really* listen to what you have to say?" For customer service you could ask, "Would you like to know the secret to telling a customer that they are wrong and have them love you for it?"

10. **Use storytelling.** Parables, analogies, metaphors, and personal experiences make a powerful point. They key is to keep the story short, relevant, and relatable to your learners. Don't be afraid to share a personal story of how you failed at something. The participants may be currently dealing with the same issue. Ensure that the message of the story is clear.

6 | 10 Basics for Active Facilitators

The basic tasks of a facilitator are to keep everyone focused on the same challenge, to make sure everyone is participating, to create a safe environment where all want to contribute, and to guide the process to achieve understanding and transfer of knowledge and skills. Being a good facilitator requires "in-the-moment" skills to ensure learning occurs. No matter how experienced you are, these basics are good reminders for all of us.

1. **Set the tone.** The tone of the session is established by you and your demeanor—calm or urgent or interested or adventurous. The group will follow your mood, so if you are sarcastic and not focused, the group will not likely be productive.

2. **All together now.** Ensure that all participants understand the concepts in each module before moving on. Stay attuned to the group needs. Going too fast? Slow down. Going too slow? Stop repeating yourself and allow learning to occur at its natural pace. Pair up those who are ahead with those who are trying to catch up. Focus on the participants. Scan the classroom for cues to their energy, interests, questions, and concerns.

3. **Be open and aware.** Assess your ignorance. Admit when you are wrong, make mistakes, or do not know. It demonstrates to participants that making mistakes is part of learning. Also be aware of your own biases toward individuals or the topic. Model the same openness you are asking of participants.

4. **Balance and recognize participation.** If people are not participating, ask everyone to write their ideas on a piece of paper. This affords time for introverts to process in silence and to contribute when it is their turn. Ensure no one person is monopolizing the discussion. Use round robins to get ideas from everyone. Whether it is a smile, a nod, or a thank you, we all respond positively to appreciation.

5. **Ask questions and listen.** Use open-ended questions that start with Who, What, Where, When, Why, and How. Try asking more and telling less to shift

Ideas from Barbara Pate Glacel, The Glacel Group, and Gary Wagenheim, Wagenheim Advisory Group, Canada

the learning to participants. After asking a question, pause and listen to their answers. Listen to the first thing participants say: It's often a clue to their real issues, concerns, and questions.

6. **Demonstrate empathy and patience.**   Show empathy, positive regard, and respect for participants regardless of their perspectives. Take your time. Don't rush through your agenda. A learning path will emerge when participants are ready. Less content often means more and deeper learning.

7. **Stay on track.**   If the discussion gets off-track, suggest that the off-track topics be "parked" for a later time and guide the discussion back to the content at hand.

8. **Encourage participation.**   There is more knowledge within the group than you have. Encourage the group to share its expertise and experience throughout. You do not need to be responsible for every concept and knowledge point in the session.

9. **Curtail disruptions.**   Manage disruptions directly and wisely. Have a list (mentally or physically) of what you can do in every situation. Then take action immediately. Don't let it get out of hand.

10. **Have fun.**   "Seriously" have fun. Learning can and should be fun, engaging, and interesting. You set the tone, so smile and laugh and do not take yourself or your knowledge too seriously.

7 | 10 Tips to Become an Engaging Facilitator

"She's an engaging facilitator!" What exactly does that mean? Are you born that way? Well, you may have natural proclivity, but being more engaging is a learnable skill. Here are some actionable tips that you might try to be even more engaging (or just check off to affirm that you already are!).

1. **Be enthusiastic.** Enthusiasm is the "secret sauce" that separates the most successful people in any profession from all the rest. It's not sufficient by itself, but it is required.

2. **Be authentic.** People can smell what is fake from a mile away. You will not be able to get through to participants unless you show up as real and authentic.

3. **Show confident benevolence.** Say what? Let's break it down. Benevolence means having others' best interests in mind and approaching others with an assumption that they mean well—expecting the best of others. Confident benevolence means showing your confidence without it trumping your humility and focus on others. It means respecting your own worth while respecting others.

4. **Be approachable.** Sometimes when we are concerned about being seen as credible, we can come across as aloof, cold, self-important, or detached. So humility and an intentional focus on others' welfare will help you come across as approachable. Smile, make eye contact, and relax!

5. **Be interested to be interesting.** In our quest to be seen as experts or to gain respect, we can put excessive emphasis on what we came to share. Instead, shift your focus to the learners and activate your curiosity. Ask questions. Be genuinely interested in others' ideas, questions, objections, concerns, or perspectives. People are instantly drawn to others who show interest in them.

6. **Use self-deprecating humor.** If you show that you don't take yourself too seriously, you will allow learners to relax and take themselves a little less seriously, too. This will help them be more open to learning and experimentation and less concerned about keeping up appearances.

Ideas from Halelly Azulay, TalentGrow LLC

7. **Be congruent in body and voice.**   When we perceive a mismatch between the verbal and nonverbal message, we tend to trust the nonverbal part of the message to be more credible and trustworthy. Don't present learners with a mismatched message and let them guess what you really feel or mean. Be congruent and ensure that your words and your actions align.

8. **Be upbeat and high-energy.**   Your energy level needs to be a couple of levels above that of the participants. If you sit or feel lethargic, you can be sure that it will have a contagion effect on the learners. Ensure that you exude lots of energy to help learners feel energized. Stay standing, keep moving, and be high-energy.

9. **Be trustworthy.**   Learners will need to show vulnerability and even share personal or uncomfortable stories or examples in order to truly grow and learn. The more you convey that you can be trusted to keep confidences and honor their trust in you, the less learners will feel at risk and the better able they will be to take chances and go outside their comfort zone, where real learning takes place.

10. **Be open to feedback.**   Actively solicit feedback from learners and not just on the "smiley sheet" at the end of the session. Ask after lunch or at the end of the first day or the morning of the second day: "What should I keep doing? What else can I do to make this a successful and comfortable learning environment for you?" Listen openly and attentively to their feedback and, as much as possible, demonstrate that you are taking it to heart by implementing changes in the course that make sense.

8   10 Tips to Keep Learners Focused

We are all busy and have lots of things on our minds. Anyone can be distracted while participating in a training session, whether in a classroom or virtual setting. Use these tips to help participants maintain their focus.

1. **Write it out.**   Give participants two to three minutes to write down everything that could distract them in the session so it's out of their heads. You could provide paper sandwich bags and suggest that they put their distractions inside to "bag them."

2. **Assigned roles.**   When working in teams or small groups, assign each team member a role, such as scribe, timekeeper, facilitator, or spokesperson. Keep the groups small enough so that no one can "drop out."

3. **Round robin.**   Go around the room or use the phone to ask each person to provide input on a specific topic; don't move on until each person has contributed.

4. **Ground rules.**   Establish ground rules for greater focus with input from the participants, such as putting phones on silent or vibrate.

5. **Individual work.**   Incorporate individual activities while in a classroom environment so participants see their fellow learners working quietly and can follow suit.

6. **Polling.**   Take instant polls or surveys to keep participants engaged in the learning content.

7. **Publicize breaks.**   Let participants know up front when session breaks will occur to prevent worrying about when they'll be able to check messages.

8. **Self-documentation.**   Ask open-ended discussion questions. Have virtual participants use whiteboard tools and classroom learners use flipcharts to document their responses.

9. **Stand and stretch.**   If energy is low, ask participants to stand up and have a stretch; if feasible, give them a fun question to ask the person next to them to boost energy.

10. **Mix it up.**   If participants have been working with the same people for much of a session, ask them to stand up and find a different seat to change the environment and gain new perspectives.

Ideas from Lisa J. Downs, DevelopmentWise Consulting

9　10 Presenting Mistakes to Avoid and a Bonus: 10 Tactics for Professional Presenters

We all want to communicate so that others will listen. We also probably all know what we could do better. This list of the mistakes most often committed by presenters will be a good reminder for what to work on during your next presentation. This list comes with a bonus! Following the mistakes is a list of reminders of what to do better.

1. **Speaking too fast.**　To shorten your speech, don't just talk faster. Make fewer points. Or, if you are given less time than promised, remove some of the quotes you are using first. Then, take out the statistics and finally the stories.

2. **Walking aimlessly.**　Move with intention and to make a point. You appear more confident when you are "standing your ground."

3. **Using verbal fillers.**　"Um" or "you know" can be distracting. Eliminating these unnecessary words takes awareness and practice. Most people don't realize they are saying them until they watch a replay. Focus on how you feel when you are about to say, "um" and try to fill that space with a pause where you say nothing at all.

4. **Swaying or shifting weight.**　Steady yourself and have good posture to present powerfully.

5. **Avoiding eye contact.**　To have a better audience connection, look at individuals seated in different areas of the room and speak directly to each as if you were having a conversation.

6. **Using a fig leaf stance.**　When you cover your body, you give a signal that you are protecting yourself or are not at ease. Instead, move your arms, use appropriate gestures, and show you are open and in control.

7. **Killing with PowerPoint.**　People prefer larger fonts and bullet points to text-heavy visuals. If you can use a picture that tells the story, that's even better.

8. **Using acronyms or jargon.**　Use real words and proper names to ensure your message is clear. Provide definitions where necessary.

Ideas from Linda Swindling, *Journey On! Training and Development,* and Lorri Allen, *Good News!*

9. **Speaking too softly.**   If a microphone is available, use it. Don't say, "Oh, I can talk loud enough." Use a microphone when necessary and practice using it. Test every microphone before you use it.

10. **Apologizing or making excuses.**   Resist the urge to save face by saying, "I'm sorry I didn't have time to prepare for this," or "I'm just going to wing this because my PowerPoint isn't working." Statements like this insult your audience and you'll lose people immediately.

To avoid these speaker mistakes and speak more confidently, remember:

1. **Know your beginning and closing cold.**   Anticipate potential questions that people may have during your presentation and address them with your speaking points.

2. **Start on time, end on time.**   Know what content and stories you can cut ahead of time to stay on schedule.

3. **Send a positive message.**   Before you begin, remind yourself that your information is important. Tell yourself, "People can't wait to hear what I have to say." Research your audience so you can tailor your content. Find out the audience size, demographics, key personnel, words that are taboo, current issues the group is facing, and so forth.

4. **Don't bluff.**   Instead say, "I don't know," or throw the question to the audience.

5. **Collect and use relevant quotes to support your points.**

6. **Tell stories to help people remember.**

7. **Use props and visual aids.**   Good use of visuals adds depth to your content. They should be simple and consistent. Always have a backup in case the room won't accommodate your visuals or in case of a technical glitch.

8. **Involve the audience with interactive activities, discussions, or questions.** But never end with Q and A. Always reserve time to conclude and close powerfully.

9. **Help people follow you by verbally giving them the structure of your speech.**

10. **End with emotion whenever possible.**   Start strong and end stronger.

10   10 Factors That Increase Retention

The speaker dropped to the floor and started doing pushups to compare the old version with the new approach. A speaker promoting nuclear disarmament dropped BBs one at a time into a tin wastebasket explaining that each BB represented a bomb or warhead the size of the Hiroshima bomb still existing today. Many were in tears two minutes later when the BBs stopped falling. A speaker pulled out a laundry basket and started folding clothes in the middle of his speech to demonstrate the idea of multitasking. Learners remember these examples years later. What can you do to create retention? How can you put that stamp of memorability on your presentation? These 10 factors will increase the magic of memorability.

1. **Primacy/Recency effect.** The brain recalls material at the beginning and at the end far better than what comes in the middle. Our most important ideas, therefore, need to be hammered home at the opening and closing.

2. **Linking.** Connect major points of a presentation with some common image or verbal marker, that is, "I have a dream that…" repeated with each new point.

3. **Outstandingness.** Your content will stick in the minds of your learners if you connect it with something unusual, strange, or out of context. Learners remember laundry being folded or BBs dropping for years. Presenters usually don't do that sort of thing.

4. **Contrast.** To increase retention, set a pattern and then disrupt it. For example, you may have four to five slides with detailed analysis. Disrupt the pattern. Your learners' minds become more alert because of the change. Add a video, provide an analogy, add graphics, or encourage audience participation. There's a boost of energy and retention,

5. **The art and energy of story.** We are hardwired to listen for stories. We are able to visualize and experience the content in our minds. A simple statement like, "That's the data but here's what happened with our number one client…," perks up our ears.

Ideas from Mary McGlynn, PowerSpeaking, Inc.

6. **Illustrate content with descriptive gestures.**   You can use your body as a visual aid. Make lists, show time progression, and illustrate scale (large and small numbers, for example) with your hands.

7. **Boost your confidence pose.**   Amy Cuddy's research at the Harvard Business School suggests that if you stand for two minutes in a "power pose," stretching out into all your personal space, you'll lower the stress hormone cortisol in your system and feel more courageous. When you look confident, the learners relax and get into the groove of your content.

8. **Use the B key.**   If you use slides, a good way to transition from one idea to another is to hit the "B" button to make the screen go blank. This breaks up the pattern and brings attention back to you. When you're ready to continue, hit "B" again and go back to the slides.

9. **Connection.**   Be interesting. Build connections. Care about your learners. Focus on them, their needs, and their motivation to be there. Have them participate.

10. **Review.**   The memory pattern will be strengthened by reinforcement. This is why a summary at the end is so critical to long-term retention.

11 | 10 Storytelling Tips

Storytelling is an effective way to help learners remember, to transform abstract concepts into understandable ideas, and to make a point without offending. The best speakers tell great stories. Tell stories to begin a training session, to explain points throughout your material, and to successfully summarize at the conclusion. Stories are especially important to break up intense data-filled sessions. Ask participants to explain how the information has helped them, and you will often hear a great story that you can share at a future training session. Some storytellers are born, but most of us get better by sticking to a few guidelines.

1. **Tell the whole story.**   A story must have a beginning, middle, and an end. Think of compelling commercials that present a problem and a solution in 30 seconds.

2. **Add surprise.**   Humor or suspense keeps people listening. Even your favorite family stories are retold because there's a twist.

3. **Keep it personal.**   Your real, personal stories are most authentic and interesting to others. People will engage when you are vulnerable, but make sure you are not the hero of every story. That makes you look arrogant.

4. **Tell new stories.**   Avoid stories told too often like the ones about the starfish or the lighthouse. Everyone has read them or heard them. You will come across as lazy or a plagiarist. If you do share someone else's story, make sure you have permission and give credit to that person.

5. **Keep it short.**   Aim for economy of words. The fewer wasted words, the bigger the impact. Minds can wander if you give too many details.

6. **Show the story.**   Use movement, vocal variety, and exaggerated facial expressions to grab attention. Remember how Robin Williams engaged us with different accents and funny faces?

7. **Hold the punchline.**   Don't get ahead of yourself. Save the punchline until the end. And be careful with humor because it is subjective. One type of humor that is always safe is self-deprecation. Audiences love it when you can laugh at yourself.

Ideas from Lorri Allen, the Soundbite Coach, *Good News!*

8. **Just say it.**   Don't preface your story with phrases such as, "Here's a story you will like" or "Now I'm going to tell you a story." Just tell it.

9. **Practice.**   Tell your story to people before you take it into the classroom. Stories get better as you see the reaction to them. You will learn where to pause to let material sink in, and you will realize some parts are not essential to get the point.

10. **Make up names.**   If you can't use names and situations for confidentiality reasons, try changing the people into talking animals, like Aesop's fables.

12 10 Tips to Effectively Launch a Practice Activity

Practice is critical for the transfer of learning to behavior. Learners need an opportunity to apply a new skill or technique in a safe environment where they will receive feedback.

1. **State the purpose.** Communicate how learners might use this skill or technique on the job. The purpose establishes relevance and value.

2. **Assign teams first.** Establish teams or partners before starting the activity. Allow people time to arrange themselves prior to offering instructions or distributing materials.

3. **Manage time.** Make the amount of time for the activity visible to all using a clock or electronic countdown timer.

4. **Prepare and label materials.** Organize materials so that everything is ready to go in advance. Include written instructions. Verbal instructions are difficult to remember and to hear in a group setting.

5. **Test your instructions.** Verify that the steps you provide make sense and nothing is missing. Complete a dry run with colleagues before the training session.

6. **Communicate to all.** Based on learning styles, learners may need you to state, write and/or demonstrate how the activity is to be conducted.

7. **Prepare the learners.** Provide a brief verbal overview of the activity that might include the purpose, time, materials, instructions, or other information. Allow questions by asking, "What questions do you have?"

8. **Monitor the practice.** Walk among the groups to provide support, answer questions, and ensure the teams are on the right track.

9. **Countdown.** Provide time checks such as, "You should be half way through," or "You should be starting on the third section," or "There are three minutes left to finish up."

10. **Debrief.** Prepare questions that guide learners to reflect on the practice and state how they will apply what they learned. Ask questions about what happened, how it relates to the workplace, and what they will do differently as a result of what they learned.

Ideas from Kimberly Seeger, MS, CPLP, Senior Talent Development Leader

13   10 Ways to Encourage Participant Timeliness

Getting the learners to return from breaks and lunch can be a struggle. It is important to make attendance expectations clear from the start, as well as model the appropriate behavior yourself. These tips will introduce some fun ways to encourage participants to return on time.

1. **Ground rules.** Establish ground rules at the beginning of the session and ask participants how they would like to handle people returning late from breaks. Past suggestions include singing, telling a joke, or donating $1 to a charity jar. The ideas need to come from the participants and they need to agree to the rules so there is buy-in. Doing nothing is also an option, since people returning late already have missed out on the content.

2. **Odd times.** Give breaks in unusual time increments. Instead of 10 or 15 minutes, people are more likely to remember and adhere to 11 or 17 minutes.

3. **Gamble for time.** Give a participant two or three dice and have them roll for the break time. Any roll under six is awarded a minimum six-minute break.

4. **Trivia.** Post a trivia question on a flipchart or PowerPoint slide and promise to show the answer after break.

5. **Comedy routine.** Tell the first half of a joke and promise the punchline when break is over.

6. **The puzzler.** Post a puzzle on a flipchart or PowerPoint and promise to show the answer after break.

7. **Team experience.** Assign participants to workgroups for the length of the class. Give teams points for participation in activities and for returning on time. If one member of the team is late, the whole team is not awarded points for that break. Teams can use their points in the end for prizes or an auction.

8. **Best is after break.** Make the opening of class after the break meaningful. Simply jump into important material as soon as the break is over.

9. **Rest of the story.** Use intriguing transitions that build curiosity by using a statement or asking a question that excites the learners to want to know more.

Ideas from Rachel Stromberg, Mad Cowford Improv

For example, in a customer service workshop, ask, "Would you like to know the secret to telling a customer that they are wrong and have them love you for it? You will be enlightened when you return from break."

10. **Reward timeliness.**   State that everyone who returns from lunch on time will be emailed a link to an article that is relevant to the course topic, or will be given one of the assessment questions in advance to help them prepare.

14   10 Creative Strategies for Forming Groups

Working in small groups is an important part of active learning. They provide an opportunity for more people to have more "air time" to express opinions and ask questions. Small groups allow learners to receive feedback more quickly and to learn from each other. Small groups create opportunities for more people to practice skills. Learning becomes more dynamic and active in small groups. Groups should vary in composition and size throughout the session. These creative strategies also add some fun. Think ahead. Do you need a certain number of people in each group? For example, do you need two people to conduct the activity and one person to observe? Or is it important to have a certain number of groups to ensure enough equipment is available? Once you know the answer to these questions, you can select a creative way to form groups.

1. **It's in the cards.**   Use children's playing cards such as "Go Fish" or "Old Maid." Ask participants to find others with similar cards. Use playing cards and ask participants to form subgroups by suit or number. Groups can be reformed again using suit or number, whichever was not used the first time.

2. **Famous names.**   Create nametags of recognizable characters for the group such as sports superstars, television characters, cartoon characters, or political figures. Learners can find the same character or complete a group, such as everyone who stars in the same TV program.

3. **Color matches.**   Use colored index cards with questions for reviewing content. Ask participants to find others with the same color card, or form a rainbow and then proceed to review course content.

4. **Bake a cookie.**   Identify key ingredients for making a chocolate chip cookie and put one or two ingredients on each index card. Ask participants to form teams so they make a complete cookie. You can serve cookies during the activity.

5. **Build it and they will come.**   Provide a different color LEGO piece(s) to each participant. Ask them to form teams based on the color and then proceed to build something.

Ideas from Gale J. Mote, Gale Mote Associates

6. Longevity line.   Ask participants to form a line around the room based on seniority with the organization. Then count off to the number of subgroups required. They could also form the line based on the month and day of their birthday.

7. Sticker it up.   Use stickers on index cards. Ask participants to find others with similar stickers. A question on the index card might be used as an icebreaker, team building exercise, or content review.

8. Jingle jangle.   Using index cards, put one to three words (depends on group size required) to several favorite jingles or familiar quotes. Ask team members to join together to complete the jingle or quote. You can make the quotes relevant to course content. You could ask the teams to sing the jingle once in place.

9. Chew team.   Provide a different piece of gum at each participant's place. Ask them to form teams such as all "Juicy Fruit" or all "bubble gum."

10. Count off.   Of course you can always count off. But you could do it in a unique way: backwards or using only even numbers. You could also ask groups to count in a foreign language. Use someone from the participant group who knows a foreign language to lead.

15   10 Options to Motivate Learners

Getting the learners engaged in the learning can be a challenge. Adult learners attend training for a variety of reasons. They attend for personal growth or career advancement, to build social relationships, or because it was expected by a manager or required for continued employment. These tips will help you gain learner buy-in and motivation to learn.

1. **Why are you here?**   Identify why they are taking the class and what they hope to gain. This will allow you to stress the components of the course that are most relevant to them.

2. **Atta boy.**   Provide frequent feedback and encouragement. Coach them with constructive suggestions for improvement and provide positive reinforcement. Simple statements like "Great question," "You're on the right track," and "I agree" allow adults to feel safe to contribute ideas and answers in front of their peers.

3. **Vary the design.**   Use a variety of teaching strategies to appeal to all learning styles.

4. **Address their needs.**   Be flexible and willing to go a little off the agenda to answer questions or meet a learning need that is relevant to the topic. Table questions that are too far off topic and address them during break, after class, or with a follow up email.

5. **Tap into their expertise.**   Acknowledge your own knowledge limitations and leverage the knowledge and experience of the participants. Even if you are highly knowledgeable about the topic, draw upon the expertise of the learners whenever possible.

6. **Idea exchanges.**   Provide opportunities for participants to exchange ideas and learn from each other. Conduct pair shares, group activities, and group discussions.

7. **Personalize.**   Allow learners to personalize the training by providing general guidelines, then allowing participants to customize projects/activities according

Ideas from Rachel Stromberg, Mad Cowford Improv

to their own learning needs or how they feel they would apply the concepts in the real world.

8. **Treat them as adults.**   Understand that adult learners have multiple responsibilities. Allow for reasonable tardiness returning from breaks to address business or personal concerns.

9. **Ask for feedback.**   Invite feedback from the participants regarding the content, activities, and the instructor.

10. **Follow up.**   Keep them engaged after the training by emailing them bonus material after the class is over, such as links to relevant online articles or a list of book recommendations.

16 10 Quick Recap Strategies

One of the advantages of classroom training is the opportunity to summarize and recap what was learned in creative ways. Recapping content helps to ensure that skills and knowledge will be transferred and applied in the workplace.

1. **Three-peat.** Have participants form triads and identify the session's three most important learning points. Have them share those insights with three other teams.

2. **Game changer.** In pairs, have participants share one behavioral change related to the training that would make the biggest difference in their work performance.

3. **Countdown.** Ask participants to write the following on an index card: three key points they want to remember, two actions to which they'll commit, and one skill they will teach to someone else.

4. **Short and tweet.** Ask participants to pair up and develop a summary of the training content using only 140 characters.

5. **60 minutes.** Ask participants to identify a skill introduced in the training to which they will devote one hour of practice during the next week.

6. **A different world.** Ask participants to imagine what their work lives would be like if they made progress on some key aspect of the training. Have each participant share his/her vision with one or two partners.

7. **Double trouble.** Have participants share two challenges they will face in the future that will require them to demonstrate the skills covered in the training. Have them share their challenges with a partner, along with the action steps they will take to address them.

8. **One and done.** Ask participants to summarize the training session in just one sentence. Have each participant share his/her summary with a partner.

9. **It's a mystery!** Ask participants to identify one area of content that remains unclear. Encourage a post-program web search to deepen their knowledge.

10. **Cheat sheet.** Have each participant write three learning points on a Post-it note. Have them attach their notes to the cover of their handouts for easy recall.

Ideas from Mark Isabella, Isabella & Associates

17   10-Step Process to Increase Applicability

To enhance the immediate usefulness and applicability of key learnings gained from development sessions, session participants do what we call "Make It Real…Fast."

1. **Pre-work.** Require each participant to come prepared with at least one real-world challenge applicable to the development session.

2. **Icebreaker.** To enable the session participants to better know and trust one another, ask each one to briefly answer an intriguing question requiring some vulnerability, such as "Who has been the most influential person in your life, and why?"

3. **Ensure confidentiality.** Set a ground rule to help facilitate real conversations. Ensure others feel safe in being vulnerable and in sharing real-life scenarios.

4. **Integrated conversations.** Within the development session, specifically take time for facilitated conversations in which participants publicly discuss their challenges with other participants.

5. **Seek feedback.** Allow participants to give each other feedback and generate ideas. This crucial input can help break initial assumptions and inspire new solutions.

6. **New approaches.** Based on the collective input, ask participants to think about how/what they would do differently.

7. **Commit in writing.** Ask each participant to create a written action plan and timeline for addressing the challenge discussed with instructions to be specific on what will be done differently.

8. **Share with group.** Each participant shares a summary of his/her action plan with other session participants. This builds accountability through transparency.

9. **Peer coaching.** If culturally appropriate, suggest that participants exchange contact information, to facilitate post-session follow-up among participants.

10. **Measure success.** After an appropriate time frame, have participants send updates on their progress and challenges. What learning was most relevant? What helped inspire their changes? What assistance do they still need?

Ideas from Kevin Louiselle, Ph.D., MDA Leadership Consulting

18   10 Ideas to Ensure Transferability

Even though some transfer of learning barriers may not be yours to resolve, you can still do your part to ensure transfer of learning. The more options you exercise, the better chances your learners have to transfer what they learned.

1. **Five tactics.** Table groups create a list of five highly effective tactics to use in applying their new skill.

2. **Two by two support.** Participants list two people and two resources they will use to support their transfer and application of skills and knowledge.

3. **Partnerships.** Participants find a partner in the workshop, and make an appointment to follow up in 10 days.

4. **Script it.** Participants create a script for a discussion with their manager outlining what they intend to do differently and what support they will require from their manager.

5. **No nos.** Table groups provide five examples of what not to do, and how to avoid those.

6. **Follow-up discussion.** Provide a schedule and signup sheet for participants to join a follow-up discussion to discuss successes and challenges of application.

7. **Interview.** Participants interview someone who has already had successful experiences with the new skills.

8. **What worked; what didn't.** Let participants know that as follow-up they will submit a one-paragraph description of how they applied the skill and what worked/what was problematic. Then a compiled list is sent to all.

9. **Results online.** Create an online share space for participants to tell about the impact of their applications.

10. **Help line.** Provide a dial-in help line scheduled for certain hours of the week with experienced professionals handling the calls.

Ideas from Wendy Axelrod, Talent Savvy Manager, LLC

19   10 Ways to Address Challenging Situations

No matter how well prepared you are, problems may occur. You cannot think of everything. It's not that a challenge arose; it's how you manage the challenge that counts. Your participants will be watching you as a role model, because they respect your ability to address anything!

1. **Room is not conducive to learning.**   Although you should always check out your room the day before, this may not be feasible. You may not see your room until an hour before your session starts, and find that it has inadequate or inappropriate furniture, is too noisy, or too small. Call the person in charge immediately. If nothing can be changed before your opening, put the learners in a small group activity and make a couple of phone calls. In the meantime make do with what you have. Find other locations for breakout sessions; going outdoors is even a possibility. You can challenge the group to identify solutions, too.

2. **Equipment fails.**   Yep, another time when you need to be prepared. Always double-check the equipment the day before when possible. Have the name and cellphone number of the person responsible for equipment handy. Follow a process to locate the issue, for example, everything plugged in and turned on? Cables firmly connected? Tried to reboot? Have a backup plan for how to substitute a flipchart for your colorful PowerPoint slides or how to create a role play instead of viewing a YouTube video. Be positive. Don't complain. Keep moving forward with your active training plan.

3. **Participant side conversations are disruptive.**   Try to prevent this by establishing ground rules. Let the group establish their own to increase ownership. Reward and model appropriate behavior. If two participants are talking, make eye contact or walk toward them while continuing your discussion or delivery. If possible casually saunter behind them and continue to talk to the group over their personal conversation. Give these folks the benefit of the doubt. They may be discussing a point you were trying to make.

4. **One participant dominates discussion or creates another disruption.**   Break eye contact with the individual and call on others by name. Hold your hand up and state that you'd like to hear from another person. Ignoring disruptive behavior is one way to manage it. You may wish to ignore most things the first time.

When it is repetitive and interferes with others' learning, you do need to take control. In some cases you can redirect a response to another learner. You can reference the ground rules. You can also change activities from large group discussions to small groups. Sometimes humor works. If none of these work, speak with the person during a break, explaining what you observe and what needs to change.

5. **Learners are not participating.**   Begin the session by ensuring that everyone speaks once or twice during the opening. Ask easier questions earlier in your session. Use a round robin to ensure that everyone knows they will need to share their thoughts. Allow the introverts time to think and prepare their response by asking everyone to write the answer to your question before discussion occurs.

6. **You lost your place.**   Take a sip of water while checking your notes. If appropriate, you can pause and ask what questions they have at this point. No one knows exactly what you were going to do or say, so it is unlikely that anyone will notice the shift. Try repeating the last point in a different way or give an example to give you time to think. You can always just admit that you forgot; few learners will be upset.

7. **Energy is down.**   Be prepared with your favorite energizer from this book or others. Move people into an activity that has them standing. Move people around into small groups with people at different tables or with those with whom they have not worked. Take a break. Create a challenge (the first team to name all 10 listening skills) or hold a competition (a relay race to list critical leadership competencies on a flipchart).

8. **A difficult group.**   If you've done all the up-front work to understand the group's needs, be certain they know what's in it for them to attend this session. How will it make their jobs easier? How will their performance improve? Why does the organization need them to have these skills? Be sure that you have established your credibility. You can try to probe one of the friendlier faces during a break; don't bury yourself in the content. You may need to address it in the session by asking, "The group seems preoccupied; is something happening that I should know?" It doesn't happen often, but when it does, it is usually best to address the issue as soon as possible.

9. **You are nervous.**   Arrive early to ground yourself with the room and make it yours. Don't try anything new—including clothes. If you have a crutch, use it,

such as having a glass of water close by. Be overly organized. During the session use up excess energy with gestures and your vocal presentation. Send a positive message: "These people are excited about learning new skills." Accept the fact that you will be nervous and know what to expect, for example, your throat will get dry, your heart races. Get your audience involved early so that the session feels like a discussion. Memorize the first 30 minutes of content. Usually nervousness dissolves after a short time. Be ultra-prepared, so that you can do the session in your sleep and practice, practice, practice.

10. **You do not feel well.**   There is little you can do about feeling under the weather. The show must go on and you probably do not have a backup trainer. Certainly if you have something contagious or are so ill that you cannot facilitate the session, you may need to cancel. It is difficult because so many other people are counting on you. Some may have traveled a long distance. If you are going to continue to conduct the training, don't tell the participants you are not feeling well. Or if you do, don't make a big deal out of it. You may get sympathy, but is that what you want? Shift the session to put even more emphasis on participant involvement. Supersize active!

20   10 Options for Active Closings

The closing of an active training session provides a sense of closure for the learners. It is a time to ensure that all expectations were met. Consider adding a closing activity that gets commitment from participants. You may also want to deliver final words of wisdom or encouragement.

1. **Action plan.**   Have participants develop an action plan. Provide a format that includes columns for the actions, starting and ending dates, resources required, and measure of success.

2. **Paired commitment.**   Have participants make a commitment to action with someone else. Ask them to exchange contact information and to call or email each other in 10 days.

3. **Email progress.**   Establish an email list where participants report their action progress to everyone in the group.

4. **Reward success.**   If you are an internal or plan a long relationship with participants, offer to send a surprise with reported action to you. You can purchase gifts from a dollar store and plan it in your budget or contract if necessary.

5. **My SMART objectives.**   Ask participants to write SMART objectives for their action and share them with the rest of the group to generate ideas for others with less grasp of application.

6. **Partner planning.**   Allow learners to pair up with anyone of their choice to create plans and to support each other with ideas.

7. **Memo to me.**   Ask each participant to write a memo to him/herself identifying what will be completed within the month. Have participants seal the memo in an envelope and address it to themselves. Gather the sealed memos and mail them to participants in 30 days.

8. **Expert support.**   Have each participant create an action plan. Once it is finished have them circulate among other participants to gather email addresses of those who can provide them with expert support and answers as they implement their action plans.

Ideas from Kenneth Stein, EdD, CPLP, SPHR, Successful Endeavors

9. **Read me a story.**   Identify a children's book that helps to close out a topic. *Oh the Places You Will Go* by Dr. Seuss works for many. Sit in a circle and have participants take turns reading the book. Discuss the implications of the book and how it relates to how participants intend to apply what they have learned.

10. **Dear Boss.**   Ask participants to write a letter to their bosses telling them what they learned and how they would like to implement what they learned. The letters are not actually sent, but they can serve as a good outline for what each learner may wish to discuss with his/her boss.

Open Every Session Actively

Icebreakers and Introductions

Involve participants right from the start. You know that you have only one time to make a first impression, so how you begin your learning event is important. Ice breakers or introductions should relate to the topic of the session. You won't find many "shoulds" or "musts" in this book, but this is one of them. Time in the classroom is too precious to spend on items that are not related to the topic. Yes it takes more time to design and customize an opening activity, but it will pay off in the end. You will see that the activities in this section are easily customizable to your content.

Your opening will get you off to a great start if you attend to several other things too. Introductions are important, and a part of learning who is attending is to learn what they know and what they need to know about the topic. Build in an element of surprise to stimulate interest and get them excited to be there. Get participants up and moving around early. The activities in this section can help you set the stage. They send a message that active participation is the norm.

1 Finding People Alike

_____ **Overview** _____

This strategy is used as a classroom introduction to help learners get to know each other quickly.

Participants

15 to 40 in most learning situations

Procedure

1. Project the 12 zodiac signs on the screen (or distribute handouts). Ask learners to identify the zodiac sign to which they belong.

2. Ask everyone to find the other participants in the classroom who were born during the same zodiac period and form small groups.

3. If the size of any group is less than three, have them join another small group.

4. Ask each group to introduce themselves and select a spokesperson. Ask the groups to name their group, identify their own group characteristics, and list their expectations of the session. Allow about 10 minutes depending upon the size of the groups.

5. Call time and ask each spokesperson to introduce the name of the group, the meaning of their zodiac symbol, its characteristics, and their expectations of the session.

Debrief

A debrief isn't necessary; however, if you wish you may use these:

1. How did your group connect? Did it have anything to do with the zodiac sign?

Contributed by George Limin Gu, Shanghai Performance Improvement Management Consulting Co., China

2. Does your zodiac sign have anything to do with what or how you prefer to learn? Why do you say that?

3. How did this activity help to start the session?

Variations

1. You could identify two to three volunteers to be the symbol masters to summarize group characteristics.

2. During the session relate the group characteristics to engage the entire class to participate.

3. Time permitting, the groups could also draw a group logo or a mascot.

4. The larger the class the better the effects of this icebreaker.

Case Example

In an ISD certification class in Shanghai, there were about 35 participants. In China, zodiac symbols can be replaced with popular animal symbols for the year the participants were born. There are 12 animal symbols to form a 12-year cycle in the Chinese calendar: Rat, Ox, Tiger, Hare, Dragon, Snake, Horse, Goat, Monkey, Rooster, Dog, and Boar. The group formed quickly by the animal symbol of the year they were born. Each group named themselves, drew the animal as their mascot, and identified the characteristics. Some of the participants knew each other but they were never grouped this way. So it was full of fun from the start to the end. The icebreaker took 20 minutes, but the effects lasted the entire four days of the class.

2 | Me in 20 Words or Less

Overview

A session opener for meetings, team building, or training that introduces participants and encourages involvement.

Participants

Activity is suitable for employees and managers, or groups comprised of both, and works with groups from 5 to 500 (large sized groups will require a room where participants are seated at small tables or can be divided into small groups quickly and easily).

Procedure

1. Divide the participants into small groups of five to seven. If not seated at tables, ask participants to arrange their chairs in a circle.

2. Prepare in advance on 3″ × 5″ index cards a set of statements or questions—one unique question for each participant in the group. Customize the questions to fit with the objectives of the learning session, team building, or training content. Questions or statements need to be written so participants can answer in 20 words or less. For example, "Briefly describe in 20 words or less a time you had a great day at work. What made it a great day?" (Great question for a class on employee engagement).

3. Prepare a PowerPoint slide, or use a whiteboard, to provide a brief overview of the exercise.

4. Provide each small group a set of the prepared cards—one card for each participant in the group.

5. Each participant draws a card and takes a few minutes to review and think of their response.

Contributed by Bette Krakau, Krakau & Associates

6. One at a time participants introduce themselves to the small group, read their question or statement, and answer it.

7. After all participants have introduced themselves and responded to the question or statement, ask the small groups to discuss what they learned from the introductions. The debrief questions may be customized in advance for the meeting or training objectives. Examples include:

- ◆ How will the info you learned from the participants in your group be helpful for accomplishing the meeting/training objectives?

- ◆ What is one thing you learned that is unique about your group or individual participants?

- ◆ What is one thing that you learned about a participant that was new information or a surprise?

- ◆ On a scale of one to five, how comfortable were you answering your question with the group?

- ◆ What made responding comfortable? Uncomfortable?

Debrief

Conduct a large group debrief by asking two to three questions that would be aligned with the overall objectives of the meeting or learning. For example, if the meeting objectives require participants to share information with the group, or a partner, discuss the value of knowing information about others at the start of the meeting. Or, if the meeting is focused on team building, discuss the importance of learning about others to strengthen the team and enhance communication.

- How will the information you learned about participants help you with the experience in our meeting (or training)?

- How comfortable were the participants in your group with answering the questions?

- What led to feeling uncomfortable when responding? Why was it uncomfortable?

- What, if any questions or statements, were uncomfortable? Why?

- Why do you think we started the meeting (or training) with this exercise?

• What do you think may be the benefits to our meeting (or training) of opening up and sharing information about yourself?

Summarize key learning or common themes from the large group debrief. Discuss the value of the exercise to the meeting or training objectives.

Variations

1. Place a different word on the cards for each participant in the small group instead of a question or statement. Relate the words on the cards to the meeting or training objectives. Each participant shares what the word means to him/her. For example, a training class on influence skills could have these words: power, persuade, selling, or negotiate. Examples of words for a team-building session could be: mission, trust, time, communication, or conflict.

2. If the number of meeting or training participants is 12 to15 maximum, and time is not a constraint, do not divide the group into small groups and ask each participant to share their introduction and response to the question or statement with all participants.

Case Examples

1. For a leadership development training class, these questions have been used with success:
   ◆ Share a time when someone inspired or motivated you to take action.
   ◆ My one greatest strength is _____.
   ◆ If you could have lunch with one person today (dead or alive), who would it be and why?
   ◆ Who is your leadership hero? Why?
   ◆ What is one adjective that describes you?
   ◆ What do you think is one characteristic of a great boss?
   ◆ Tell us about a time when someone mentored you.
   ◆ What is one thing that excites you about attending this meeting?

2. For a team-building session, these questions have been used with success:

- Tell us about a time you were part of a high-performing team.

- What is the most trusting thing that you have done on a team?

- Share a time when you contributed to the success of a team.

- Modesty aside, what is a strength you bring to this team?

- Tell us about a time you were on a team that struggled.

- What is one adjective that you think is important to team success?

- What is one barrier to team success?

- Tell us one thing "short and sweet" about yourself.

To keep the exercise moving quickly, place on the cards, and on the PowerPoint slide or whiteboard, that participants need to respond in 20 words or less.

3 Traffic Lights

Overview

This simple yet efficient strategy helps the trainer to gauge participants' expectations regarding the upcoming training session.

Participants

5 to 50 participants

Procedure

1. Give three index cards to each participant: one green, one yellow, and one red.

2. Prepare 5 to 10 statements about the content or process of the training, one statement per slide.

3. Ask the participants to take a stance on the first statement by raising the appropriate card. Green means they agree, yellow means no opinion, and red means disagree.

4. Count and state aloud the results. If a participant shows more than one color, ask why.

5. Repeat steps three and four for every statement.

6. Sum up the conclusions and adjust the training accordingly.

Debrief

• How well have I interpreted your expectations?

• What other wishes or preferences do you have regarding the training?

Contributed by Lauri Luoto, Psycon Corp., Finland

Variations

1. Instead of statements, you can show the list of topics you are going to cover and ask the participants to indicate how relevant each topic is for them. You may ask the participants to use each color at least once in order to prevent people from giving the same answer to all questions.

2. Now that people have the cards available, it allows you to collect fast feedback throughout the delivery of the training. For example, after a group assignment you can ask if the time allowed was not enough (red), too much (green), or just right (yellow).

3. If there is a need for an icebreaker before the training, you can start with a few casual statements like "The local basketball team is going to win today's match" and ask participants to hold up a card that demonstrates how much they agree with you.

Case Examples

1. In time management training, you might use statements like these:

   ◆ Our meetings are usually very efficient (to identify the most topical time management issues).

   ◆ There has been a lot of discussion about time management in my workplace (to assess prior knowledge).

   ◆ I have been able to develop my time management skills during the last 12 months (to identify good practice).

2. In management training, you might use statements like these:

   ◆ I am working in a supervisory role (to clarify participants' current situation).

   ◆ I have or have had underperforming subordinates in my team (to identify the most topical issues).

   ◆ I have been able to implement new ideas I got from the previous training session (to evaluate participants' progress in a multiday training).

4   Honoring Experience and Expertise

Overview

Use this strategy to show participants that you honor and respect the experience that they bring to the training, and set them up for ongoing participation throughout the session.

Participants

Any number

Procedure

1. As part of participant introductions, ask each to tell you the number of years of experience they have on the job, or if leadership training, in a leadership role.

2. List the number for each on a flip chart or smart board and sum the total number of years.

3. Congratulate the group on being so experienced.

4. Tell them their experience far outweighs your own, so while you have important content to present, you will be relying on them to share their experiences, learnings, and perspectives throughout the session.

Debrief

- What do you notice about the range of experience on our list? (Note especially the mix of high numbers and low numbers.)

- What can you "short-timers" expect to learn from your more experienced peers? What can you journeymen expect to learn from those newer to the role?

Contributed by Marilyn Marles, MS HRD/OD, Marles Group

- What is a challenge you face if you are relatively new in your role? What benefits do you bring?

- How can longer experience become an obstacle to effectiveness?

Variations

1. If tenure appears to align with age, use this information to discuss generational differences.

2. Create mentoring pairs based on years in the role.

3. Use years of experience as a basis for breaking into smaller groups, debrief around similarities and differences of their output.

4. You may also use this exercise to gauge how to adjust your content based on the level of expertise in the room.

Case Example

In a session on teams:

- Acknowledge the resident expertise as you introduce your training topics, and be sure to ask them for additional insights: "Based on your personal experience, how do you see respect or the lack of it affecting team performance?"

- Additional questions: "How do you ensure that both newer and more seasoned team members have an opportunity to have their ideas heard in discussions? What does it feel like when that happens?"

5   We're All in the Same Boat

────────────────── Overview ──────────────────

When you want participants to know more about each other and to recognize commonalities.

Participants

Any number in small groups of six to eight or conducted in a whole class of 20 or less

Procedure

1. Have participants begin to talk about themselves.

2. When someone has a similar experience, the individual says "Me too" and begins his/her introduction until someone else says "Me too." This continues until all members have had an opportunity to introduce themselves to the group.

3. If you have small groups, rotate individuals after five to eight minutes to allow everyone to meet as many as possible.

4. End the activity once all participants have had an opportunity to talk about themselves.

Debrief

- What did you learn that was interesting about the other participants?
- How was this exercise helpful in getting to know other people?
- What kinds of information did we share that made the greatest impression on you?

───────────────

Contributed by Dr. Kella Price, SPHR, CPLP, Price Consulting Group

Variations

1. Create a sheet to record commonalities with other participants. On the sheet, have them list the person's name and what they had in common.

2. Have participants write a little-known fact about themselves on their name tag or tent card.

Case Example

Hi, my name is Kella Price. I'm a military spouse and I live in Yuma, Arizona. I have four boys. (Tonya says "me too").

Hi, my name is Tonya. I also have four boys. I grew up in Tennessee, but I'm a Steelers fan. (Kevin says "me too").

I'm Kevin and I'm a huge Steelers fan. I went to school for Business (game continues).

Identifying Participant Expectations

C larify expectations so you and the participants know what will be covered as well as what will not be covered. This is an opportunity for you to share objectives and to learn your participants' skill and knowledge level surrounding the content. Recognizing employees for their expertise and experience can clarify that you expect them to share their knowledge with the rest of the group. Keep your eyes and ears open; this is an opportunity to clarify misperceptions and to observe how well individuals will work cooperatively during your time together. You will also learn about the attitudes participants bring with them into the learning session. Use the activities in this section to learn what your participants want to learn!

6 On Course, of Course

Overview

Participants select a topic that interests them, identify their expectations, and work with the same group at various times during the learning session.

Participants

This exercise works with any size group and any type of employee. It serves as an excellent icebreaker for those who don't know each other well.

Procedure

1. Identify the main objectives or topics of the course to be presented and post flipchart pages with one topic written at the top of each.

2. As participants enter, ask them to circulate around the room, read the posted objectives on the flip chart sheets, and then sign their name on the one that most interests them.

3. Once the session begins, review the agenda and explain the intent of each objective/topic.

4. Ask participants to go to the page where they signed their name and list:

    ♦ Why the topic was of interest

    ♦ What they hope to learn about the topic

5. Allow about 5–10 minutes. Once each group has finished its list, rotate through the pages having each group report out.

6. After each of the topics has been covered, debrief using some of the questions listed.

Contributed by Marlene Caroselli, Center for Professional Development

7. Throughout the session ask the topic groups to regroup for special assignments, activities, or just because you need the same number of small groups. You can announce with great fanfare, "And what do our (topic) experts have to report?"

Debrief

- You've just heard what interests participants about each topic/objective; what questions do you have about any of the topics? (If possible, allow the group to respond.)
- What can others share about this topic/objective?
- After addressing one of the topics/objectives, ask if the topic is more or less interesting and why.

Variations

1. If no one signs one of the charts, respond to the questions yourself by stating why the topic is interesting and why it should be to each participant. Share some of the things they will address in the learning session.

2. You could define spaces where participants sign their names by allotting a maximum number for each topic; for example, if you have five objectives and 25 participants you might allow only five or six people to sign up for each topic.

3. As a summary, ask table groups to write one thing they learned about each of the topics. Then go around the room, calling on each table group in turn to share one learned fact or insight about each of the topics.

Case Example

When using this concept for a class lasting only four hours, the process changes slightly. Post these questions on flipchart sheets, in lieu of course objectives. Participants write an answer but do not sign their names. Use the charts to review what you will or will not cover in the short time.

- What would you like to learn about this topic?
- What is one thing you already know about this topic?
- What puzzles you about this topic?
- How will this topic benefit you on your job?

7 Ask and Deliver

_____ **Overview** _____

Use this strategy to open and close your session. Learn the expectations your participants have for their learning experience. At the end come full circle and ask whether their expectations have been met.

Participants

No limit or requirements

Procedure

1. Assign participants to small groups: four to six recommended. Give each group markers and flipchart paper.

2. Tell them that the groups will be given a question to answer and that they are to record answers on the flipchart sheet.

3. Ask the groups, "What is it about (SUBJECT MATTER OF TRAINING) that drives you crazy? What makes it really hard?" Allow about 10 minutes.

4. As each group finishes, have them post their flipchart sheet on the wall.

5. Have each group send one person to their sheet to present for the group, with a marker in hand.

6. Choose the longest list and have the group presenter read through their responses. Ask all other presenters to check off anything that the first presenter covers and instruct them that they will not have to repeat what has already been stated.

7. Continue presenter by presenter until all ideas have been stated (continue to check off duplicate ideas). As ideas are presented, silently take note of what you have already planned to cover in the session. Verbally acknowledge with a comment like "That's a good one!"

Contributed by Lorna J. Kibbey, Kibbey Leadership Solutions

8. Quickly explain why subjects are not relevant to your content for anything that comes up that you had not planned to cover (or take note to adjust during the session).

9. At the end of the session, ask groups to review their list to ensure that all of their expectations were met. You should be at 100 percent every time based on the opening. Participants will be excited that you covered all of their issues.

Debrief

Open

- How surprised are you that so many of you share the same frustrations?
- Do you feel better knowing that others share many of the challenges you face?

Close

- How did we do? Did we give you some tips for dealing with the challenges you face?

Variations

1. If the group is not very large, let each group present their list and verbally acknowledge duplicates.

2. You could report lists in a round robin with participants checking off each item as they hear it.

3. To save time, ask the group to agree on their top three to five.

4. The closing activity can be expanded to give the group time to discuss the challenges covered on their list. It can be shortened by asking for a quick thumbs-up or thumbs-down, group-by-group.

5. If the group brings up topics that really should be covered and you had not planned for them, tell participants that you will send information out after the session.

Case Examples

1. In a session to teach communication skills, use this prompt: "Discuss your most challenging communication encounters. In other words, what really drives you crazy in talking with other people?" At the end of the session use this prompt: "Back to the beginning! Did we cover your most challenging communication encounters?"

2. In a session on business writing, use this prompt: "Discuss your most aggravating challenges when dealing with written documents. In other words, what really drives you crazy?" At the end of the session use this prompt: "Back to the beginning! Did we cover your most aggravating challenges?"

3. In a session on middle management skills, use this prompt: "What is hard about being a middle-manager? What is it that drives you crazy?" At the end use this prompt: "Back to the beginning! Did we cover your challenges?"

8   Visualizing Success

Overview

Use this activity to promote ownership by the learner of their experience, and to encourage active engagement throughout the training.

Participants

This activity works for most classroom groups of up to 15 participants. See variations for larger groups.

Procedure

1. After introductory classroom material, provide each participant with one piece of flipchart paper and a marker and instruct the participants that they will be creating a "Success Mind-Map" on their flipchart.

2. Each participant should think of the most critical piece of knowledge, new skill, or improvement that they could gain as a result of this session. They write that idea in the middle of the flipchart and put a circle around it. Allow five minutes.

3. Instruct the group to think about the strategies they could use during the session to make sure they reach their goal. This could include activities (role-plays, taking notes), perspective (being open to new ideas, listening to peers), or any other ways to prepare themselves for achieving their goal (review notes after class each night, asking a peer in the classroom to be an accountability partner after the class). Allow 15 minutes.

4. At the end of allotted time, ask each participant to share some of the ideas they have written.

Contributed by Jennifer Labin, TERP Associates

5. Throughout the session, before each break or at regular intervals, instruct participants to return to their chart. They can check off strategies, add notes, or in any way review the ideas to keep their awareness focused.

6. At the end of the session, have each participant create one to three action items to further their development on their stated goal.

Debrief

- What inspired you to choose the goal you set?
- What ideas did you get from others in the room?
- How did this chart help you keep focused on your goal throughout the session?

Variations

1. For larger groups, ask for two or three volunteers to share their charts rather than the entire group.

2. Provide a template in the participant workbook and have participants work privately.

Case Example

This method has worked particularly well for leadership development workshops, and other sessions where the outcomes are individualized. In a leadership development setting with midlevel managers, participants were able to customize their experience based on their unique situations and perspectives. It also encouraged networking between participants when they could see others that had common goals or different strengths.

9   Why Are You Here?

Overview

This activity can be used to kick off a learning session and allow the facilitator to tailor the content of the session to the participants and their interest or goals.

Participants

You can do this as a whole group, or assign the participants to groups of four to six.

Procedure

1. Split the participants if desired using any number of techniques to have them move around. The smaller groups will enable more interaction.

2. Ask, "What do you want to learn today? What is your goal for this session?"

3. Allow time for individuals to write down their own goals; have them share the goals with the group.

4. In the large group ask them to share common themes. You may wish to record them on a flipchart.

5. Compare participant needs with the session learning objectives.

6. Use the list as a closing tool once the learning session is complete. Look at the chart. Review items on the list and ask the audience, "What did you learn about this? What was a key point about (topic)?"

Debrief

Opening
• What common themes emerged?
• What unique outliers do we see?

Contributed by Dr. Kella Price, SPHR, CPLP, Price Consulting Group

Closing

- What did you learn about this?
- What was a key point about (topic)?
- What concept that we discussed today challenged you?
- What are resources and tools that can provide you with more information about (topic)?

Variations

Have participants create a knowledge question about subject items. Number these items, and place these questions within the groups to assess their knowledge. Have each group rotate through the questions, and discuss the answers.

1. Be sure if a topic is mentioned at the beginning of this activity that is beyond the scope of the learning session; tell the audience that the topic will not be discussed. Try to refer them to resources on that topic after the session is over.
2. You can use Twitter to collect audience responses as well. This can be helpful in a large group to get additional feedback and allow interaction without participants physically moving from their seats.

Case Example

Figure 3.1 is an example of a question posed to a large group at a conference to obtain a large number of responses in a short amount of time. Participants who did not have a Twitter account were asked to share their ideas with someone nearby who did.

Figure 3.1

10 Topic Networking

Overview

Use this strategy to connect learners to each other, what they already know about the training topic, and what they hope to learn. It serves to inform the trainer of participants' attitudes and feelings toward the topic. It is also helpful to gain buy-in from participants who are required to attend the training.

Participants

12 to 40 in most learning situations

Procedure

1. Round 1: Find people who like the same junk food (or any other fun topic) and form a group of three or more people. Discuss three or more things you already know about the training topic with your group. Circulate through the groups to help them get started if they are stuck or if they are still talking about their favorite junk foods.

2. After three to five minutes, ask the groups to take turns reporting out some of their discussion points.

3. Round 2: Find people who like the same genre of movie (or any other fun topic) you do and form a group of three or more people. Discuss how you feel about the training topic with your group.

4. After three to five minutes, ask the groups to take turns reporting out some of their discussion points.

5. Round 3: Find people who have the same kind of pet you do (or no pets) and form a group of three to five people. Discuss why you are attending this training and what you hope to learn.

Contributed by Rachel Stromberg, Mad Cowford Improv

6. After three to five minutes, ask the groups to take turns reporting some of their discussion points.

7. Capture what they hope to learn on a flipchart and post it on the wall.

Debrief

- What common themes did you discover that others knew or wanted to learn?
- What ideas were shared that you'd like to try yourself?
- How was talking about what you already know relevant to today's session?

Variations

1. Use this activity in a variety of courses or with a variety of discussion topics as it works for practically all topics.

2. Be creative in selecting topics to get people into their breakout groups (favorite candy, class in high school, author, Beatles song, local restaurant, or others).

3. Use a soft cushy ball for the participants to toss from group to group to give responses.

4. For larger groups it is effective to list each topic and instructions on a PowerPoint slide.

5. If too many people form a group to have an effective discussion, ask them to break out by subtopic; for example, if 12 people form a group because they like dogs, ask them to divide into smaller groups based on a preference for big dogs or little dogs, long- or short-haired dogs.

Case Examples

In a session on performance management you could use these topics:

- Discuss what you already know about setting and measuring goals.
- Discuss what you already know about conducting an annual review meeting with an employee.
- Discuss the challenges you face when rating an employee's performance.

In a session on business writing you could use these topics:

- Discuss what pet peeves you have about other people's emails.
- Discuss your best tips for editing your writing.
- Discuss the challenges you face when writing a proposal.

11   Different Question, Same Result

Overview

A creative lively way to ensure that participants meet others while answering different questions to identify their expectations.

Participants

Any number, the more the merrier, for any topic; however, a number over 25 may take a significant time to debrief.

Procedure

1. Create index cards with one question written on each. See the Case Examples or create your own. Create enough so that every person has one card and that there are at least two or three of each of the selected question.

2. Hand an index card to each learner. Have them find others who have the same question. Once they form their group, have them respond to the question jotting their answers on the index cards. Allow about 10 minutes for this step.

3. Call time out, and ask each group to announce its question and their responses to it.

4. Capture responses that identify participant expectations on a flipchart page. Post the chart page on the wall to remind you and the participants of their expectations.

Debrief

- What common themes did you discover that others knew or wanted to learn?
- How could we ask different questions and still reach a common goal of identifying expectations?
- What ideas were shared that you wish you had thought of and mentioned?

Variations

1. Limit the number of questions to reduce the time.

2. You may name the subtopics on the cards if you wish.

Case Example

Each person receives one question and there is at least one other person who has the same card. For example, if you have a class of 20 participants, you would select a maximum of 10 questions so a pair of participants would have the same question. If you select five questions, create four index cards of each for the 20 participants.

Possible questions for the index cards:

- Why did you choose this class?
- Why are you here?
- What questions about (topic) do you have?
- What advice or information do you want to gain?
- What skills do you hope to acquire?
- What advice, information, or skills don't you need or want?
- Name one thing you want to take back to the workplace.
- What are your hopes for this learning session?
- What are your concerns for this learning session?
- What is the one "must have" that you need from this learning session?
- What are your expectations?
- What have you learned from previous classes on this topic?
- What experience do you have around this topic?

Delivering Active Learning

Connecting Learning to the Workplace

This section contains techniques that can be used throughout a learning session. It is critical that you tie the content to the real world. Connecting learning to the workplace helps participants recognize what's in it for them, addresses their perceived challenges, and also raises their confidence to make changes based on their newly acquired skills and knowledge. The activities in this section remind learners that it's all about what they take back to the workplace that counts. It is critical to connect training content to the actual work learners are expected to perform back on the job. Ultimately, when done right, participants' managers will see changed behaviors, practiced skills, and improved attitudes. Both activities in this section help ensure the learning session content is connected to the workplace.

12   Advice Exchange

Overview

Use this strategy to prepare participants to apply a skill they have learned. This helps them address their perceived greatest challenges, while also raising confidence about the challenges where they already have expertise.

Participants

Groupings of three to five people, addressing approximately five different challenges, for a total of up to 25 can be conducted in classroom settings, or virtually if breakout rooms are available.

Procedure

1. Set up the space with five flipchart stands or blank whiteboards, each with an application challenge listed at the top. (Challenges are identified in advance by the workshop designer, leaving one open chart for the participants to identify and add to the set.)

2. Briefly discuss that when applying a new skill, there is often a gap between "knowing" and "doing." Becoming proficient at doing requires addressing application challenges.

3. Ask groups to select one of the challenges where they feel they have the most expertise: one chart per group.

4. Groups work at the chart listing all their advice for addressing the challenge, based on successes they have had or they have observed. To wrap up their discussion, they circle the two most crucial pieces of advice.

5. Each group presents the two most crucial pieces of advice to others.

6. After all the group debriefs, more advice may be added via a prepared handout.

Contributed by Wendy Axelrod, Talent Savvy Manager, LLC

Debrief

Debrief with the entire workshop after individual team reports.

- What are examples of how you might encounter this challenge?
- What are the advantages of using the advice provided? What modifications, if any, would you need to make to ensure this worked well?

Variation

1. When there is sufficient time, provide actual content (in a handout) about how to address the challenge or have the participants research their chosen challenge online for a more powerful report out.
2. One or two more challenges can be added if the group is slightly larger, or a second set of these groupings can be used for even larger meetings.
3. Allow individuals to self-select a challenge, defining a maximum number of individuals who can work in a group.

Case Example

In a "Leading Effective Meetings" seminar for managers in an international pharmaceutical company, participants explored how to manage facilitation challenges while keeping the tone of the meeting positive. In trios, they selected one of the following common facilitation challenges and identified best tactics to address them based on their experience or observing others.

- Keep participants engaged.
- Address when group goes off on a tangent.
- Manage time allocations.
- Manage participants who are challenging.
- Keep group from getting bogged down.

After all groups presented their reports, the facilitator provided more content to round out the discussions. Here's an example of content in one handout:

"How to Address a Group That Goes Off on a Tangent"

- Gently remind them of the objectives and expected results of the meeting.
- Summarize key points made.
- Ask the group if it is possible to move on and handle this item later.
- Put the off-target item on follow-up list (parking lot).
- Ensure the item receives follow-up attention.

13   Pull Up a Chair

Overview

It is critical to connect training content to the actual work learners are expected to perform back on the job. Instead of plowing through content, it is important for the facilitator to pause at key points along the way to help participants make these connections. To implement this strategy, the facilitator "pulls up a chair" (PUC) and poses questions to the group as to how they will actually use or apply what they are learning, and what outcomes they would expect from these efforts.

Participants

Unlimited number of participants; PUC works equally well with classroom and live online training.

Procedure

1. Ideally, PUC moments are built into the program in advance. This tactic can also be used ad hoc when you sense that participants do not understand how they might use the content in their everyday work.

2. To initiate a PUC moment, pause during your delivery of content or immediately following an activity related to a key program takeaway or objective.

3. Tell the group that it is time to discuss what has just transpired in relation to participants' actual work.

4. Ask one or more questions of the group such as, "How might you apply what we just covered when you get back to work?" or "What barriers might you face when you try to apply what we just covered?" or "When you perform these skills on the job, what types of responses do you anticipate receiving?"

Contributed by Wendy and Jim Kirkpatrick, Kirkpatrick Partners

5. Allow participants to voice concerns and objections, as well as positive responses. Call on the group to identify solutions to barriers and opportunities to leverage successes. After a few minutes of discussion, summarize action points and close the discussion, so participants feel that they were heard, and they know what to do.

Debrief

The debriefing is wrapped into the activity. Simply ensure that the learners feel comfortable responding to a summary question such as, "What will you do as a result of this discussion?"

Case Examples

1. When training a group of new supervisors in a two-day classroom setting, PUC questions you might ask along the way include:

   ♦ "How are you feeling about performing this new role?"

   ♦ "What challenges do you think you will face as you move from the role of employee to supervisor?"

   ♦ "What kind of results do you anticipate from your efforts?"

2. When developing an asynchronous e-learning program on customer service, questions you might embed into the course include:

   ♦ "How do you plan to apply the concept of profiling customers' complaints?"

   ♦ "What barriers do you anticipate facing when you use this new system?"

   ♦ "What additional help will you need to be successful in your role as a customer service associate?"

Engaging Participants in Learning

Engaging participants in what they are learning is critical because engagement leads to learning. Having a number of techniques available to you is a great way to ensure that you will achieve the engagement (and ultimately the learning) that you require. How do you do that? Initially participants expect you to take the lead in a learning session. You need to shift the focus away from your role as a leader and to your role as a facilitator as quickly as you can. Your behavior will also encourage or discourage engagement. Engagement is not designed as "activity" only. Participants need to be engaged in discussions as well. Be sure that you listen well, accept input, ask questions, encourage questions, and know when to practice silence. Your goal is to increase engagement and participation—if not, why are they called "participants?" The activities in this section will have your participants engaged physically and mentally.

14   Four Corners

Overview

> This learning strategy surfaces issues and challenges regarding the topic at the
> outset of the learning experience so that all participants can provide their input.
> It allows the proverbial "elephants in the room" to be revealed and discussed,
> allowing participants to understand more fully the challenges involved to open
> their minds to learning the skillset and mindset required to be effective in a
> topic area.

Participants

Any classroom size will work, but it is most effective to have 20–24 participants to
ensure four levels of opinions; too few people won't provide the potential opinion
differences desired.

Procedure

1. Create three or four controversial and provocative statements about the topic area
   to get varying opinions from participants about the extent to which they agree or
   disagree with them.

2. Place a flipchart in each of the four corners of the room. On the front page of each
   flipchart write in large letters one of the following: "Strongly Agree," "Agree,"
   "Disagree," "Strongly Disagree." Tear off these four pages and put them on the
   wall closest to their respective flipcharts.

3. Show the first provocative statement on a slide.

4. Have participants react to the statement by moving to the corner of the room
   that represents their own opinions about the statement. A well-written statement
   is likely to get at least some who agree and some who disagree with it. All four
   corners do not need to be represented, but there should be some differences of
   opinion.

Contributed by Dr. Stephen L. Cohen, Strategic Leadership Collaborative

5. Once participants have reached their respective corners, have them discuss why they are there as opposed to any of the other corners. Have them list their reasons on the flip chart.

6. After 5 to 10 minutes, have each corner explain their point of view. If a debate occurs, facilitate the differences. Continue the discussion for about 10 minutes. The goal is not to gain consensus, but to surface different points of view, which may be informative to others.

7. Repeat this process for each statement.

Debrief

- Why are you in the corner of the room you are in; that is, why have you reacted to the statement the way you have?

- What are the reasons you decided to be there as opposed to any of the other three corners?

- What have you learned based on your and your colleagues' responses to the statements posed?

Variations

1. The key to effectiveness is to be sure the statements that are presented are provocative and controversial enough to get participants to have different opinions based on their own experiences. Ensure that you understand the resistance and/or support for the statements that may exist for the group.

2. Test each statement before "going live" in the classroom. If, for example, there is little to no variance with the responses to the statements, new statements need to be created.

Case Example

A company was having trouble getting more of its managers to take the performance appraisal process seriously as they either waited to the very last minute to complete them, or didn't do them at all. As a result, they created a two-day workshop to help these managers not only understand the importance of the process for developing their employees, but also to provide them with the skills necessary to carry out the process, including giving feedback.

They used four statements which were:

1. The most technically proficient individual contributors in our company are more likely to become the good managers.

2. Our managers develop their teams to behave with a broad view, putting the company's needs first, even if it is at the expense of their immediate unit's needs.

3. Our managers are the people most responsible for developing their direct reports.

4. It doesn't really matter how you are evaluated around here, since it is simply who you know that gets you ahead.

The four corners activity was used at the outset of the workshop to surface some of these issues and learn why there was so much resistance to the process. These four statements resulted in the intended disparity of opinion, but this doesn't mean they would work for another company. Each organization has its own culture and values and that's why it is important to create new statements each time.

15 | Create a Timeline

Overview

Use a timeline of events as an alternative to presenting facts to a group.

Participants

No specific requirements and any number

Procedure

1. Create flip charts with the decades as titles (1960s, 1970s, 1980s).
2. Create note cards or Post-Its, each listing one event. Use key facts that people need to know, for example, company history for new hires (acquisitions or products).
3. Do not include the year with the description. Have an answer sheet of each fact and the date.
4. Distribute the note cards among the group and ask them to sequence and post the facts on appropriate decade flipchart.
5. Make any adjustments as needed to the information to get it correct.
6. Ask for volunteers to present the information to the class.

Debrief

- What surprised you the most during this activity?
- How does knowing these dates affect what you do?

Variations

1. The information may be given as pre-reading.
2. This can be done as teams, with multiple sets of note cards and flip charts.

Contributed by Renie McClay, Inspired Learning, LLC

3. You may wish to use spray adhesive on the flip charts allowing the index cards to be easily posted and repositioned if necessary.

4. Timelines can be captured on computers.

Case Example

This activity was used with a food manufacturing company with this timeline.

1950s

1951   Started making spaghetti sauce and pasta in Mama's kitchen

1959   Started selling at the corner grocery store

1960s

1962   Gained first major account and sold in supermarkets

1967   Purchased a manufacturing facility and became Mama's Sauce and Pasta

1969   Created company slogan "Just Like Mama Made"

1970s

1971   Acquired a noodle company and began the brand Noodles for Dinner

1975   Hired sales force and began national expansion

1980s

1985   Was in the top three brands in the US

1986   Company went public

1988   Introduced the Just Add Meat boxed dinners

1990s

1990   Expanded sales to Canada

1997   Brought the All-Italian brand to the United States

2000s

2004   Introduced a Pasta Fast entrée line

2001   Created the 10 Minute Meal Ideas promotion and website

16 Make Your Case

Overview

This learning strategy can be used anytime there may be different points of view among participants. It gets people moving and provides an opportunity to demonstrate important interpersonal team and leadership skills such as being authentic and vulnerable, building trust, being influential, and storytelling depending on the focus you choose.

Participants

5 to 50 participants, allowing enough space for adequate movement

Procedure

1. Create a handout with four to eight controversial statements or questions based on the topic. Distribute this handout to all participants and ask them to complete their handout. Use questions they can answer with "agree/disagree" or "fair/unfair" or "acceptable/not acceptable" or "positive/negative."

2. Pose the first statement or question to the group.

3. Assign one end of the room one of the responses, for example, fair, and the other end of the room the opposite response, for example, unfair. Ask all of the participants to stand up at the same time and go to the place in the room that best aligns with their position/opinion on the topic. They take their handouts along.

4. Allow time for the participants in each defined group to mingle among themselves and identify common ground. Ask each group to make their case. Encourage them to use examples (without names) or stories to help persuade others to see and understand their point of view.

Contributed by Gale J. Mote, Gale Mote Associates

5. Begin with the group with fewer members. Ask a spokesperson to summarize how and why the group feels the way they do. Tell them to make their case.

6. Invite participants in the other group to physically move if they feel their opinion has changed based on the points being shared.

7. Invite the second group to make their case. If time allows, it is good to allow for clarifying questions and rebuttal among the groups.

8. Go through each of the statements on the handout in the same way.

Debrief

Select the most appropriate based on the purpose of the activity.

- How did you feel when you were first asked to stand up and move? Afraid? Nervous? Hesitant? Confident? To what do you attribute your emotional state at the time?

- How did it feel to be in the minority? (In teams, fear of separation and being the only one often leads to groupthink or "going along to get along." It is important to emphasize the importance of being true to one's own feelings and beliefs.)

- How did it feel to be in the majority? What effect, if any, did the size of the groups have on how members made their case?

- What did you learn from the "cases" that were made among the various groups? What does this tell us about the importance of understanding the real needs and interests of a position in resolving conflict, solving problems, and making decisions?

- Did you physically change your opinion and location in the room? How do you feel about changing your point of view? (In teaming, when everyone participates openly, higher quality decisions are made with more commitment and ownership. All must remain open to ensure that everyone's perspective is heard, considered, and understood.)

- What would be necessary to get the entire room standing all together at the end of the exercise?

Variations

1. When participants are completing the handout, you may invite them to also write down their opinions that support the reasoning behind their response.

2. If participants refuse to move to one of the identified areas, allow them to stand where they are comfortable and continue to include them in the conversations by asking for their rationale.

3. Be watchful of participants who seem hesitant to move to a minority position. Quietly move along side them and ask if you can be of help. Remind everyone that their opinion is as valid and true as everyone else's in the room.

4. This exercise is great in building trust and demonstrating vulnerability. It requires participants to openly share their real feelings.

5. You might pair one person from each opposing group together to discuss their varying points of view. This only works well when the groups seem to be about evenly split.

Case Example

A trainer uses this exercise with new first-line supervisors to examine the issue of trust. A key element is treating employees fairly. However, many supervisors have different beliefs and interpretations about behaviors and decisions that are fair. This leads to a lack of trust not only with direct reports but among peers. Supervisors often complain about other supervisors who are not "following the procedures" or who "pick and choose how to enforce the rules."

- The trainer developed a handout of eight scenarios that describe relevant supervisor behaviors that may be construed by some as fair and others as unfair. As an example, a supervisor does not assign attendance points to a direct report who has excellent quality and productivity.

- Participants review the scenarios and respond with a "fair" or "unfair" on the handout. Participants write down any notes on the reasoning behind their points of view and do not share their responses during this time.

- Participants move to "fair" or "unfair." based on their response to the first scenario and each group is invited to make its case.

- The groups are asked: "Why did they believe the situation was fair or unfair? What did they believe was right or wrong about the supervisor's behavior? What affect did the behavior have on employee and peer relationships?"

Note: This is a variation of Mel's learning strategy, "Go to Your Post" (*101 Ways to Make Training Active*, Second Edition). It is also a twist on Sharon Bowman's "Take a Stand" (*The Ten Minute Trainer—150 Ways to Teach it Quick and Make it Stick*).

17 The Power of Demonstration Learning

Overview

Use this strategy to share principles or techniques through rich dialogue. It allows participants to engage with the topic and to experience the value of the principles or techniques.

Participants

4 to 40 in most situations

Procedure

1. Determine the principles or techniques you wish participants to learn about your topic.

2. Create a scenario in which you, as the facilitator, will display some of those principles or techniques and in which you will violate others.

3. After the scenario, ask participants to describe what you did well and what you didn't do so well that you could improve. Write their responses on a flipchart.

4. Compare their responses to the list you've already prepared, highlighting any that they didn't notice and discuss.

Debrief

- How does the scenario we just enacted in this room replicate scenarios you're in back on the job?

- What do you want to remember about this experience when you're back at work?

- When I ignored some of the principles or techniques on this list during the demonstration, what was the result or impact? What was the result or impact when I embraced them?

Contributed by Sophie Oberstein, New York University

- How have you seen some effective individuals use the principles or strategies I did well? How have you seen some ineffective individuals violate the principles or strategies as I did?

- What will you do differently as a result of this demonstration and discussion?

Variations

1. While the procedure above does not include telling participants before the scenario what you are going to be doing, you can also tell the group before you begin that you are about to do a demonstration of some things one should and some things one should not do in regards to your topic. Ask them to take notes during the demonstration of what you do well and what you could improve in order to discuss it afterwards.

2. You can also ask for their feedback on your demonstration as you go along so that you can improve in the ways that they suggest as you go. For instance, if you were trying to explain the posture one needs to display to impress someone during a job interview, sit in a chair slumped over and looking into your lap and ask them to call out suggestions that would "fix" you into a more impressive posture.

Case Examples

1. When trying to share the principles of giving good feedback, you could have a participant stand up and deliver a one-minute speech (You'd write the speech in advance and give it to her to read off of an index card). Afterwards, give the feedback, "That was excellent, Jane. Thanks for sharing." Then ask the group what was effective about that feedback and how it could be improved.

2. When trying to show participants in a leadership program what you need to do to build trust, you could ask two volunteers to gain your trust so that you will allow them to blindfold you in front of the group and guide you in taking a crumpled ball of paper all the way across the room to the trash can in the back. Ask the remaining participants to take note of what the two volunteers did to gain your trust.

3. When trying to help participants come up with techniques for managing a Q&A period during their presentations, you can first conduct a mock Q&A session by distributing some prepared questions on cards to random participants in the room. Ask everyone else to note how your responses to the questions worked and how they did not work.

18   Twitter Engagement

Overview

Most participants in learning sessions bring their smartphones and tablets to learning events. Instead of prohibiting use of the devices, or worrying about them using the devices to text, surf, or scan their Facebook, give them activities to engage and interact through the learning session.

Participants

This will work best with participants who are already using Twitter, although providing a tutorial and instructions on how to set up prior to the class is helpful. Review the expectations for tweeting at the beginning of class.

Procedure

1. Select and communicate a hashtag for the training session.

2. Create visuals that call attention to the hashtag and include "tweetable phrases" of 140 characters or less.

3. When you want the audience to specifically respond on Twitter, post the question on the slide with the Twitter bird and hashtag. Ask the question live and discuss, but encourage those using Twitter to respond there. Participants who are reluctant to speak up in a large group may be more likely to participate online.

4. Some examples of when you'd incorporate Twitter to get audience engaged in conversation live and online:

   ◆ Pre-session survey questions

   ◆ Icebreaker introductions

   ◆ Discussion questions

   ◆ Polls and checking understanding questions

   ◆ Summaries of key learnings

Contributed by Dr. Kella Price, SPHR, CPLP, Price Consulting Group

Debrief

- What key points from today's session did we capture on Twitter?
- What elements of today's training resonated with you?
- What can you go back to the job and implement right away?

Variations

1. If all participants do not already use Twitter, provide a tutorial and instructions on how to set up prior to the class. In addition, it is important to review the expectations for tweeting at the beginning of the learning session.

2. If possible, collect Twitter usernames during the registration process so that you can include them on nametags, as well as create a list for the learning event to send them targeted pre-session information or content.

3. A social media team onsite during the training can be helpful to post tweets, monitor the feed, and answer questions.

4. Periodically show the backchannel during the training session. Call out key learnings, as well as point out and answer questions.

Case Example

During a presentation the speaker asked, "What types of surveys would benefit from using a QR Code?" Responses on twitter included:

- Employee satisfaction surveys
- Exit survey
- Customer performance
- Testing, evaluating, polling
- Name tags

19   Photo Environment Survey

Overview

Use this activity to incorporate visuals as a point of discussion for a variety of topics.

Participants

No specifications in a classroom or online

Procedure

1. Set up an area for group to post pictures, for example, Group intranet, SharePoint site, Facebook group page, Pinterest board, or a blog page. (Social sites can be set to be private and invitation only if concerned about security.)

2. Alternatively, the group members can send pictures directly to you to load into any of the places previously mentioned.

3. Send directions to the group one or two weeks weeks prior to the session to take a picture of any area of the business which supports the topic of your learning session. For example, if you are conducting a culture workshop, you could ask for examples that would encourage or discourage a team culture such as: spaces for collaboration, hallway discussions, an inviting break area, a group of smiling faces, a picture of cubicles populated with people with headphones, closed doors, screen shot of "access blocked," or a "no loud talking" sign.

4. Present the pictures during the appropriate segment to create discussion.

5. At the end of the session you may wish to send the link of the photos to anyone in the organization who might have the ability to make changes or appreciate reinforcement.

Contributed by Shannon Tipton, Learning Rebels

Debrief

Ask questions related specifically to the learning session. In the case of the team culture you could ask:

- How did you feel taking these pictures? How did it reinforce your belief of a team environment?
- What did this exercise tell you about how you interact with the team?
- What gaps exist between where we think we are and what we are actually doing? What can we do about it?
- Based on this experience, how can you improve the teamwork in your department/group/division?
- If you were to ask other people in the organization to complete this exercise, what do you think the results would be?

Variations

1. Use a before and after—take the pictures now and take pictures again in six months to determine if change has occurred.
2. Categorize pictures based on organization position. For example, have pictures submitted by front line, managers, corporate office, and then review the differences.

Case Examples

1. Can be used as a customer service survey: Take pictures supporting or disproving a customer service mentality.
2. Can be used to develop/revise a mission statement: Take pictures of parts of the business which support the mission statement and pictures taken of the outside world that best visually represent the organization.

Note: This exercise was inspired by an example in *Social Media for Trainers* by Jane Bozarth.

20   ### Learning at-a-Glance Placemat

Overview

Make your training stand out from the sea of 8 1/2 × 11 paper and PowerPoint slides with a placemat for notes and activities. The part "Info Graphic" and part "Roadmap" of the entire course is on one page.

Participants

No requirements in either a classroom setting or with some preplanning for an e-learning situation.

Procedure

1. Once you develop your course, identify the major themes throughout it. Determine what sections participants will most likely take notes. How many module/topic areas are there? What activities will they need to write responses? Divide a 12″ × 18″ or 11″ × 17″ page of paper (depending on your printer/copier's capabilities) into the number of topic areas you need. Distill the key points of the lesson onto one page—like a "placemat."

2. Design the placemat into a roadmap so participants can visually tell where the starting point is and create a logical flow of topic. Incorporate key pictures and graphics used in the PowerPoint slides into the placemat so that it ties together and provides the participant a visual reference as they follow along in the course.

Contributed by Mark Boccia, Marriott International

3. Leave space for "key takeaways" or other notes.

4. Consider the flipside of the page for all of the activities and the front-side for all of the essential course content.

Debrief

You can ask participants to look at the whole picture and summarize the content of the course, using their placemat as visual reference. This helps both the instructional designer and ultimately the participant to see the course at once… including how the topics weave together and build on each other to create the "story."

Variations

1. Ideally, the placemat is designed so participants can take it back home and tack it up on the wall for visual reference. Now your course becomes top-of-mind instead of simply a workbook placed on the bookshelf. The key success is the larger paper that signals "this is something different" from binders and other smaller job aids that are typically distributed.

2. An optional activity is to have the participants sketch their own infographic on the blank flipside of their placement, especially if there are modules or topics that are dense with information.

3. A fully developed placemat can be produced, laminated, and then placed on the participants' tables for reference, with one side being completely dedicated to a game or activity that the table groups need to reference.

Case Example

The example in Figures 5.1 and 5.2 was used in a class to teach the realities of business, introducing tools employees could use to help them make decisions.

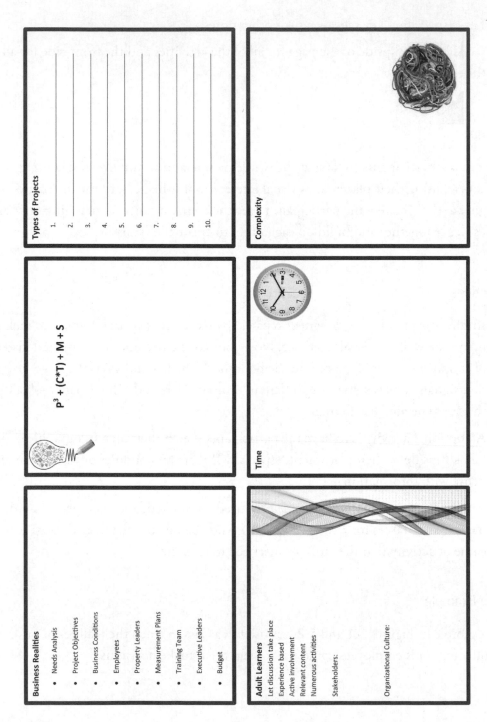

Figure 5.1

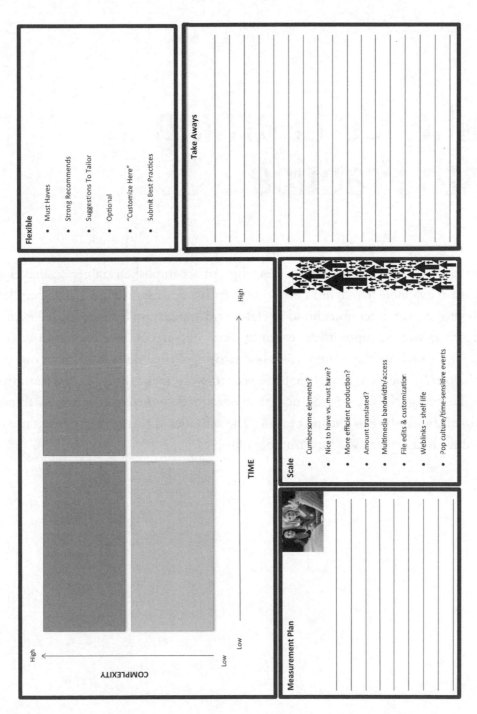

Figure 5.2

Enhance Learning with Practice

Practice is the best way to enable learning. An accomplished trainer ensures that time is available to practice new skills to ensure success once the participant leaves the classroom. A trainer must build in real-world application by using actual examples that learners will face upon their return to the workplace. Be sure enough time is available throughout the session. It is good to bring several skills together in one practice session. In addition, ensure that it is acceptable to make mistakes and learn from them. Learning in a safe environment where feedback and coaching are available is comforting and a productive use of time. The activities in this section present methods to practice that can be used for a number of topics.

21   Shine a Light on Me!

_____ **Overview** _____

Use this strategy to illustrate the importance of using strong open-ended questions in any communication situation.

Participants

4 to 20 in most learning situations

Procedure

1. Teach the benefits of open-ended questions and how they elicit important information. Draw a comparison to close-ended questions. Ask for examples from
   participants.

2. If a sales situation, point out that it is the goal for the client, not the salesperson,
   to talk 80 percent of the time. Show survey data stating that clients believe "salespeople talk too much" as their number one problem. If you are teaching interview
   skills, point out that you learn more from the candidates when they are doing the
   talking.

3. Ask someone in the class if they would like to demonstrate in front of the group.
   Do not tell them what is coming. Ask another member of the class to turn out the
   lights in the room. Sit face-to-face in the darkly-lit room and tell the person that
   you are the buyer and need to be sold; the interviewee being interviewed for a job;
   or a communicator in any situation. Click on the flashlight, and start the role-play.

4. Proceed. If the sales trainee (interviewer) asks a good open-ended question, hold
   the flashlight above your own head, and give a lengthy answer. If the participant
   asks a closed-ended question that can be answered with a "yes, no, maybe" or a
   time/number, answer quickly and shine the flashlight over the individual's head
   when you're done. Whoever is talking is in the "spotlight." The goal is to keep the

Contributed by Joseph Anzalone, Director, Dean, College of Sales and Reservations, Hilton
Worldwide

spotlight on the client, not the salesperson; on the interviewee, not the interviewer; or on the person with the information in other communication situations.

Debrief

- Who was the light shining on most? Why?
- What types of questions seem to keep the person talking?
- What were the best questions you heard?
- How will you prepare your questions in the future?

Variations

1. This activity can be used in any communication such as an interview or a sales situation.

2. After the front of the room demonstration, pair everyone off and try it in the dark room with several flashlights. The exercise gets even more fun as the light flies around the room.

3. For extra pressure, shine the light in the salesperson's eyes. They will work hard to ask a question to get the light away from them.

4. For less pressure, use a ticking oven timer. Whoever is holding it (talking) loses!

Case Example

Open-ended questions (light mostly on the client)

- Tell me more about your company's conference.
- What do you envision this solution ideally looking like?
- Share with me some of the challenges you've had in the past with your strategic partners.

Closed-ended questions (light mostly on the salesperson)

- Are you happy with your current provider?
- Do you have a busy season?
- How many people are involved in this decision?

22   Go with the Flow

Overview

Incorporating true improvisation (improv) into a live session, this activity works well for any communications or interpersonal skills topic. A bonus list of resources is provided so you can learn more about improv.

Participants

Best for groups of 8 to 12, this strategy can be used with larger groups by identifying some participants as audience members who are coached to watch for certain things in each scene.

Procedure

1. Identify real-world scenarios to use as scene starters.

2. Show a brief clip of *Whose Line Is It Anyway?* from YouTube.

3. Explain that the participants will enter the action by tapping a player on the shoulder. That player steps out of the action, and the participant takes his or her place. You can determine and state in advance expectations such as everyone participates.

4. Select two or three participants and assign roles for the first scene.

5. Present the scene. Encourage participants to step in as the scene unfolds.

Debrief

This debriefing can be customized to elicit responses and provoke thinking around various aspects of human interaction, such as body language, tone or delivery, word choice, or specific processes and scripting for call centers or other situations.

- Tell us about your experience as the [fill in the role].
- You also played the [fill in the role], what was this like for you?

Contributed by Jo Lynn Feinstein, EdD, CPLP, DaVita–HealthCare Partners

- How did the scene change as "actors" stepped in or out?
- If some participants are audience members, ask what they noticed during the scene.

Variations

1. If participants are reluctant to step in voluntarily, ring a bell or use some other distinctive sound to announce an "actor" swap. This may require advanced identification of participants who will step into the roles upon hearing that sound.

2. Ask participants to list typical workday scenarios and/or pain points in their daily interactions. Use these as your scene starters.

3. Give role descriptions to "actors" privately and let one character respond to and identify the situation each "actor" presents. Example can be found 40 seconds into this video: https://www.youtube.com/watch?v=iCtx4sbZkyI

4. Use the following resources to learn more about improvisation:
   - Karen Hough, "Improvisation: A Radical New Way to Train," in T&D, April, 2011
   - Michelle James, "The Fertile Unknown," in Ian Gotts' & John Cremer's *Using Improv in Business,* as posted at http://iangotts.files.wordpress.com/2012/02/using-improv-in-business-e2-v1.pdf
   - Jesse Scinto, a lecturer in Columbia University's Strategic Communications programs, posted at http://www.forbes.com/sites/forbesleadershipforum/2014/06/27/why-improv-training-is-great-business-training/
   - Meredith Wood, writing for Funding Gates, posted "Management Training: Improv in the Workplace," at https://blog.fundinggates.com/2012/10/management-training-improv-workplace/
   - Mark Tutton, for CNN, posted "Why using improvisation to teach business skills is no joke," at http://www.cnn.com/2010/BUSINESS/02/18/improvisation.business.skills/

Case Example

For customer service training in a healthcare organization set the scene for participants:

- It's 8:00 PM on a Saturday. [To first "actor"] You've just come home to find your mother in bed, disoriented.
- [To second "actor"] You are working the evening shift at the Patient Support Center.
- [To first "actor"] You realize that it's Saturday night and the doctor's office isn't open. You don't think it warrants an emergency room visit, but you're not sure what to do. You call the Patient Support Center.

The "actors" take it from here. Go with whatever evolves in the scene. Other participants tap an actor on the shoulder and step into that role periodically. Stop the action and debrief the experience.

23   Show It Online

Overview

Give the audience a chance to enhance their learning about a topic by allowing them to review available video on their own devices.

Participants

No limit

Procedure

1. Divide participants into groups of four.

2. Assign a specific topic or problem statement.

3. Give a specific time in which to complete the assignment (twenty to thirty minutes recommended).

4. Instruct them to use their own devices (smartphones, tablets, iPads) to do a video search online.

5. Each group is to find a short video that they feel best enhances understanding of the topic or offers solutions to the problem statement. (Limit the video play time depending on how much time you have. It is important to set a time limit to eliminate a lot of video screening during the exercise.)

6. At the end of 20 minutes (or chosen time limit) move to debrief—use one of the variations described next.

Debrief

- Tell us about the video you selected and why you chose it. (Each group reports.)
- What were common themes in the videos you browsed? (Whole class discusses.)
- What conclusions can we draw?

Contributed by Lorna J. Kibbey, Kibbey Leadership Solutions

Variations

1. At the end of the exercise, show the video you have preselected. In the debriefing ask if any of the groups selected video with a similar theme.

2. Show a few of the videos to the group. (You can have each group send a link to you for quick loading. If the class size is small, have participants gather at each group table to watch the selected video.)

3. After participants have selected videos, have each group post the URL of the selected video on a piece of flipchart paper so that everyone can access later. (Encourage participants to take a picture of the list using their phone).

4. Set up a session on Twitter specifically for the session and have one participant from each group post their selected video there.

Case Examples

1. In a session on leadership, ask the group to find a video that gives insight into how to motivate employees. After the debriefing, show Daniel Pink's classic video "The Surprising Truth about What Motivates Us" (10.48 minutes on YouTube).

2. In a session on communication, ask the group to find video that gives insight into how people communicate and what goes wrong. After the debriefing, show "Busting the Mehrabian Myth" by Creativity Works (3.29 minutes on YouTube).

| 24 | **Two Negatives Make a Positive** |

─────────────── **Overview** ───────────────

This is an improvisation (improv) exercise best done in person, but could also be done in a chat window during a webinar or over a phone with a bit more structure.

Participants

5 to infinity

Procedure

1. Establish a problem to which the learners need to brainstorm a solution.

2. Ask participants to quickly write down a list of three to five ways that the group could make the problem worse.

3. Each person will very quickly share either a way to make the problem worse (they can't repeat one that was already said), or a way to counteract (opposite/negative) the problem just stated. For example, in a session about healthy lifestyle, the first person says "eat too much," next says "eat healthy," next says "watch too much TV," next says "go for a quick walk," and so forth. Continue stating one negative, then one positive, until everyone has had a turn. If there is an odd number, have the facilitator finish it up or ask the last person to share another positive for the last negative.

4. Explain the logistics of the exercise and what order the participants will speak. For example, you could establish a leader at every round table, and process starting with the leader to the leader's right, then go right again to the next table's leader. For classroom, you could go by rows (or columns to make it more interesting).

───────────

Contributed by Lou Russell, Russell Martin & Associates

5. Ask for a volunteer to capture the good ideas on a flipchart.

6. Split the room in half and make it a race. Time each side as they share their ideas and see which side can complete the task first.

Debrief

- From this list, what are things that you could do right now as an individual?
- From this list, what are things that you could do with your team?
- From this list, what are things that you could do with a task force?
- What are the primary benefits of solving this problem? Would it be worth it? Why?
- What personal commitment will you each make toward solving this problem? How will you measure your success?

Variations

1. Use this as an intro activity, establishing the boundaries of the issue and solution.

2. Use this as a closing activity, reviewing lessons learned and turning strategy into action.

3. Break into more than two teams for a larger group and instill competition.

4. Use this on a webinar and use the participant list to determine the order.

5. Conduct this as an email game and assign the timing (days!) to complete the activity.

Case Example

For a topic of employee engagement ask, "What are ways we can prevent or destroy employee engagement?"

Negative Statement	Negative of the Negative = Positive Statement
Create individual competition; don't encourage social connection.	Assign people to work together. Encourage social experiences regularly.
Never let people finish anything. Keep moving them to new priorities.	Give people time to get one project done before starting another.
Do not thank them for their work when they do a great job.	Catch them being good and tell them.
Constantly reinforce their weaknesses and mistakes.	Before pointing out a mistake, ask yourself is this about them (is it really that big a deal) or you (ego)?

Note: This is based on an opposite exercise from Thiagi; at some point I added the element of improv.

25   Acronym BINGO

Overview

This strategy is terrific for any subject matter that uses many acronyms. It works well for a new employee orientation, where acronyms of the entire organization are likely to be sprinkled throughout any discussion. It helps participants focus on what the speaker is saying, and makes it OK to ask questions without appearing to "not know."

Participants

Works with any size group

Procedure

1. Prepare the longest list of acronyms related to the subject matter of the course that you can compile. Be sure you can identify in words what the acronyms mean.

2. Create a table to convert the list of acronyms into BINGO cards (9, 16, or 25 squares). You may wish to create three to five versions by placing the acronyms in different locations on the table.

3. Within the first 30 minutes of the class, hand out one BINGO card to each participant. Instruct them that, anytime they hear a speaker using an acronym without first identifying what it means, they are to raise their hands and ask the speaker to explain what the acronym means.

4. As an acronym is used, if participants have that acronym on their BINGO cards, they mark it off with an "X."

5. When participants completely fill a vertical, horizontal, or diagonal row with crossed-off acronyms, they shout "BINGO."

6. The participant reads the acronyms and identifies what they mean.

Contributed by Kathy Shurte, CPLP, Florida Department of Transportation

Debrief

- Can I clarify for anyone an acronym you may have heard today that was not on your card, and was not identified by the speaker?

- Are there any acronyms on your card that we did not hear today, and you would like explained?

- When is it appropriate to use these acronyms?

- When is it not appropriate to use these acronyms?

Variations

1. "Fabulous" prizes may be awarded to winners. In New Employee Orientation, lanyards are a practical giveaway. Dollar stores are a great source of prizes.

2. You may play variations on the contiguous rows. For example, in a full day class, you may want to play "full card" BINGO, which means all the squares are marked.

3. Instead of creating a table you may use the BINGO Card Generator at www.eslactivities.com.

4. The ESL Activities site also allows you to make picture BINGO cards.

5. If your organization has a SharePoint or other site where a complete list of acronyms is located, be sure to show participants how to locate the list before leaving the class.

Case Example

FM	GIS	MOT	CPM	CBT
CTQP	FSECC	MPO	VE	EEO
PD&E	PE	ITS	NHI	PM
TC	AARF	TRESS	MFMP	CPR2
BII	DPA	EBFC	ITP	CPR

26 Sequence Is Important

Overview

Use this strategy for content that must be sequenced accurately.

Participants

Any number in small groups of three to five

Procedure

1. Write each step in a sequential process on an index card.

2. Form participant groups of three to five and give each group a set of cards.

3. Ask participant groups to sequence the steps in a logical order.

4. Ask a spokesperson to report out and explain the rationale for the order of their sequence.

5. When participants disagree on the sequence, have them identify which rationale best fits the situation. There can often be conflicting rationales. The best rationale is often the one that makes sense to the participants.

6. Summarize this activity using the debriefing question.

Debriefing

- What did you realize about this subject while working on the activity?

- What, if anything, surprised you about this subject?

- How do you see yourself using what you have learned today?

Contributed by Jean Barbazette, The Training Clinic

Variation

You could have each individual sequence the cards and then pair with someone to compare results.

Case Example

A help desk was overwhelmed with calls and realized that if they could help the workforce check out some of the most common causes of computer failures everyone would be serviced faster. A noontime brown bag session was held to explain that troubleshooting could be both fast and accurate if done in a specific sequence. The IT team went through the appropriate sequence of steps using a video format. Following the video, teams were given sets of laminated cards that had the troubleshooting steps listed. Participants were asked to put the cards in the correct sequence. Each participant was given a deck of the steps numbered in correct order to take with them as a job aid once they returned to their own computers.

Learn with Your Peers

A prerequisite for excellent trainers is a guarantee that participants learn from their peers. When a trainer recognizes this, it builds self-esteem and places the responsibility to learn and to share what they know on each participant. Malcolm Knowles, father of adult learning theory, was one of the first people to draw attention to the fact that adults come to a learning opportunity with a wealth of experience and a great deal to contribute. Trainers are successful when they identify ways to build on and make use of adults' hard-earned experience. Even the most knowledgeable learn more when sharing with their peers. It helps participants sort out what they understand, what they still need to learn, and what questions they may have as they are involved in their own learning. These strategies are practical ways to involve peers in pleasurable and productive ways.

27   Four Square and Share

Overview

Use this strategy to expand participants thinking to address an issue or apply a skill, by gaining multiple perspectives.

Participants

4 groupings of 3 to 6 people, for a total of 12 to 24; multiple sets of these 4 groupings can be used for larger meetings.

Procedure

1. Set up the space with four flipchart stands, arranged to signify four sides of a square. Leave plenty of space between and around so people can stand in front of charts and then roam to others charts.

2. Provide highlights about this issue, or application of a skill, that the group has been discussing and identify the importance of understanding this from multiple perspectives.

3. Assign one group to each of the four charts and asks them to stand by their chart.

4. Using a PowerPoint or a handout, each group is assigned their own specific perspective and two to three questions to answer from that perspective. They write their succinct responses on the flipchart (allow 5–10 minutes).

5. Once the groups have answered their questions, ask them to rotate to the chart to their left. Arriving at this (new) chart with its distinct perspective, they review what has already been written and add their own comments. Repeat the rotation to the left two more times, so that groups comment on the other three charts.

6. Now, ask the groups for one more move to the left and participants arrive at their "home base" chart. They review the additions to the chart and summarize an enhanced perspective.

7. Have each group report a summary of their chart and lessons learned.

Contributed by Wendy Axelrod, Talent Savvy Manager, LLC

Debrief

For each group report to entire workshop:

- How did your going-in assumptions about this issue (or application of this skill) change, once your assumed responsibility for your assigned perspective?
- How did the other three groups shape your further thinking about the issue (or application of the skill)?

For the entire workshop:

- In what ways is it possible to approach this issue (or application of this skill) keeping multiple perspectives in mind? Is there common ground, or is it OK to allow for four distinct perspectives?
- What would you now say are three important actions to take when addressing this issue (or applying this skill)?
- What did you learn by exploring this issue from four perspectives that will be useful in other circumstances?

Variations

1. For smaller groups, this can also work with three groups at three charts.
2. The facilitator or a handout provides the content bullets that represent the perspectives for each chart. Participant work then focuses on "given this perspective, what next steps would be appropriate?"

Case Example

In a "Professional Interactions with Customers" workshop for supervisors of an educational facility dedicated to advancing the quality of life for individuals with disabilities, Four Square and Share was used to consider the varying perspectives and needs of four stakeholder groups.

Consider how you would manage expectations of our key stakeholder groups when we announce that three long-time trusted faculty members from our Darby

School (20 percent of tenured staff from that unit) are retiring next spring, and will be replaced with newly recruited faculty. Explore this challenge from the perspective of one of the following stakeholders with whom you interact:

- Students' parents or grandparents
- Representative from a funding agency
- Speech and language therapists who work with the students and count on a special relationship with faculty members for follow-through in the classroom
- Representative from a state regulatory agency that reviews quality of programming

    Discuss the following:

- Given their vested interest in the quality of our faculty, what questions would they likely raise to you, the supervisor?
- What would be the appropriate language, tone, and demeanor to take when responding to them?

28	**Rotating Review**

Overview

Use this strategy to review assignments or class discussion points that participants have written about individually prior to class discussion. It promotes team learning and reinforces the benefits of individual work combined with group work.

Participants

4 to100 in most learning situations

Procedure

1. List topic-related questions on a flip chart, PowerPoint slide, or whiteboard if using this for class discussion points. Or if it is to review assignments, have students come to class prepared with a hard copy of their assignments. Ask participants to quietly write answers to the questions individually or take out the hard copy of their assignment.

2. After all participants have completed their answers (or have taken their assignments out), ask them to form teams of four to five.

3. Have participants pass their written responses or assignments to the person to the left. The person on the left reads the assignment and circles the most impressive aspect of the written response or assignment.

4. Have participants pass their written responses or assignments to the person to the left (it is now two people away from its owner). This person reads the assignment and draws a rectangle around the least impressive aspect of the written response or assignment.

5. Have participants pass their written responses or assignments to the person to the left (it is now three people away from its owner). This person reads the assignment and writes one change to the content to improve the response or assignment.

Contributed by Meghann L. Drury-Grogan, PhD, Fordham University

6. Pass the written response or assignment back to its original owner for review of the feedback.

7. Ask the team to discuss the feedback and why each person gave the feedback they did. Allow enough time for each person to ave a turn.

8. Ask a spokesperson from each group to summarize the feedback answers of their team, including which was the most beneficial feedback received.

Debrief

- What happened when you reviewed the response or assignment first versus after it had already been marked by reviewers?

- How did this experience help you understand the power of working individually versus a group?

- What happened in your discussion of the feedback each person provided?

- Did some feedback conflict, and if so, what did you do and discuss with your group?

- How will you use what you learned in the next week?

Variations

1. Invite the entire group to select the best piece of feedback for each response or assignment.

2. To increase feedback, add additional rounds.

3. You could conduct two rounds. The first round focuses on content and the second focuses on format.

4. With slight adjustments, this activity could focus on giving feedback instead of the actual content feedback as it is written. The debriefing would change to asking about the effectiveness of the feedback discussion.

Case Example

In a session to review an assignment of completing a resume, have participants bring in their hard copy of their resume. They each pass their resume to the person on their left in their group for review.

29 Angles, Tangles, and Dangles

Overview

> This mid-program strategy allows for a recap on what's been learned and a quick assessment of what content needs to be reinforced or explored in greater detail.

Participants

4 to 25 participants for any topic

Procedure

1. At the end of the first half of a learning program, tell participants that they will be engaging in a brief recap of what they've learned so far.

2. Reveal a flipchart page with the words, "Angles," "Tangles," and "Dangles" written on it.

3. Ask them to work with a partner for five minutes to identify items under each of these categories:
   - Angles: Ideas or concepts they now see differently as a result of what they've learned.
   - Tangles: Ideas or concepts they've discovered to be more complicated or challenging than they originally thought.
   - Dangles: Ideas or concepts that remain unclear and should be explained or explored in more detail.

Debrief

- After participants have concluded their discussions, ask volunteers to share items from their "Angles" lists.
- Next, ask two to three volunteers to identify points from the "Tangles" category.

Contributed by Mark Isabella, Isabella & Associates

- Then, have three to five participants name their "Dangle" items. Record these contributions on a flipchart.
- Tell participants that in the second half of the program, the group will spend more time clarifying the "Dangle" issues.
- Also offer group members the opportunity to discuss dangling issues with you on a break or after the learning program.

Variation

Prepare three flipchart pages, one with the word "Angles" on it, a second that says "Tangles," and a third labeled "Dangles." Ask participants to create Post-it notes for each category and place them on the appropriate pages. Have participants perform a Gallery Walk, moving from easel to easel reading the Post-it notes on each flipchart page. Poll the group on which "Dangle" items to focus on during the second half of the training.

Case Example

At the midpoint of a training session on conflict management, partners discuss program content and complete their three lists.

Volunteer participants share the following "Angle" items: One reports that the material on conflict goals changed his views of how to negotiate successfully. Another says that the conflict styles model informed her of the behavioral options available when negotiating.

Participants next share their "Tangles": One participant reports that she now sees conflict as being more complex than she once did. Another says that he realizes that he needs to plan more carefully for his negotiations.

In the "Dangles" part of the debriefing, one participant says that she's still unclear about the differences between collaboration and compromise. Another participant says that he is still unsure of how to negotiate with someone who is angry.

The facilitator promises to explore those issues in more detail before the end of the program.

Note: A variation of this procedure was included in *Mark Isabella's Engagement Emergency*, a card deck published by The Thiagi Group.

30   The Power of Story

Overview

Use this strategy to bring forth real-life experiences to demonstrate that participants already have valuable skills and knowledge on a particular subject. It reinforces strengths and opens up the opportunity to further hone a competency.

Participants

Typically 12 to 40 in most learning situations

Procedure

1. Provide a story prompt on a flip chart, PowerPoint slide, whiteboard, or in participant materials.

2. Ask participants to spend one minute reflecting on the situation that the prompt brings to mind.

3. Have participants form groups of three to four. Each person shares his/her personal story without interruption from the other small group members.

4. When all stories have been heard in the small group, have members identify in writing what they collectively learned from the situations and identify a spokesperson to share the lessons.

5. Ask the group to select one story that best exemplifies the subject.

6. Each spokesperson shares what was learned in the small group, and the selected story in each group is told to everyone in the room.

7. Summarize by asking the large group to identify any additional learnings.

Contributed by Lori L. Silverman, Partners for Progress

Debrief

- How did it feel to tell your story to others?
- What did you like about listening to stories from others?
- What are the benefits of eliciting stories from others to reinforce existing skills and knowledge?
- In the coming week, where and with whom could you elicit a story to strengthen what the person/group already knows?

Variations

1. Pairs can be used instead of groups of three to four participants.
2. Instead of having the small groups identify learnings, facilitate this collectively in the larger group.
3. To save time, you do not need to have the small groups select a story to be retold to everyone.
4. To save time, instead of asking each small group to identify one story to be retold, ask the large group if they heard a story that really stood out for them and needs to be heard by everyone.

Case Examples

1. In new hire orientation, instead of presenting information on the organization's core values, use story prompts written specifically to draw out the essence of each one. Examples:

   ◆ Tell me about a time in your career when you received an unrealistic urgent request and you found a way to successfully handle it.

   ◆ Tell me about a situation where you offered your assistance to someone at work and it really made a difference.

   ◆ Tell me about a time when you received appreciation for a job well done beyond a mere "thank you" that made a significant and lasting impact on you.

2. In a customer service workshop you could use these story prompts:

- ◆ Tell me about a situation when you successfully dealt with an extremely difficult customer.

- ◆ Tell me about a time when you were a difficult customer, and someone very effectively dealt with the situation on your behalf.

3. In a staff meeting to promote engagement you could use these story prompts:

- ◆ Tell me about that moment when you knew this was the perfect career path (job) for you.

- ◆ Tell me about a work situation that to this day makes you say, "I made the right career choice."

31   QR Code Query

Overview

> Participants use their mobile devices and QR Codes to review content and discuss in small groups. This activity works best in the physical classroom.

Participants

Works with any knowledge level and has been conducted with 9 to 350 participants

Procedure

1. Divide your core message into steps, questions, or individual pieces.

2. Access a free QR Code generator such as http://qrcode.kaywa.com/ and add the information to the QR Code. Use one code per step, question, or piece of content.

3. Print the QR Codes and place them on flipchart pages around the room.

4. Have participants divide into small discussion groups with at least one mobile device and a free QR Code reader installed. Assign one group per flipchart.

5. Ask each group to scan their code, discuss their content, and make notes on the flipchart.

6. Rotate the groups around the room to different QR Codes to collect different views on each part. All groups do not have to visit every flipchart.

7. Wrap up the activity by having groups report out what they learned at each code.

Debrief

- What new information did you learn at each code?
- What do you still need to know?

Contributed by Larry Straining, CPLP, Larry's Training LLC

Variations

1. Break a process down into steps. Put each step into a QR Code.

2. Pose different solutions to a problem. Place each solution into a QR Code.

Case Example

Participants watch a series of videos that are linked to the QR code (possibly a longer video broken into smaller sections). When we begin, the groups scan the QR Code and watch the video. In this case each group rotates until each group has watched every video. This creates small discussion groups around the key topics.

32   Peer Assessment

Overview

Use this strategy to deliver "data dump" type content in a fun and challenging way. It is also a helpful activity when you are given little or no time to learn the topic you have been asked to teach.

Participants

10 to 25 in most learning situations

Procedure

1. Divide participants into teams of three to five people.

2. Assign each team a segment of the content.

3. Instruct them to create three to five questions for another team based on their segment of content. They write each question on a 3″ × 5″ card, one question per card. They also create one card as their "master" card that lists all their questions and answers. Tell them they have 10 minutes.

4. Ask the teams to swap cards with a different team who will research the answers to the questions on the cards from the other team. Allow 10 minutes for this.

5. Bring the group together and have each team share questions and answers. Ask the team that created the questions to validate that the answers are correct.

6. Fill in any blanks if important content is omitted from the questions or lead further discussions on the topic when appropriate.

Debrief

- What new or surprising information did you gain from your research?
- What did you learn that wasn't one of the questions you wrote or looked up?
- What topics would you like to know more about?

Submitted by Rachel Stromberg, Mad Cowford Improv

Variation

1. As a review activity:

♦ Give all participants two sticky notes and ask them to write a question they still have about the content or a question they think will stump their peers.

♦ Ask them to post their questions on the wall in the front of the room.

♦ Have them take two questions that are not theirs and go back to their materials and find the answers.

♦ Conduct a round robin of the questions and answers.

2. As a content activity it works well to assign sections of policy in an employee handbook for new hires, an introduction to a contract for sales training, and highly detailed and dry content on product descriptions for sales and customer service training.)

Case Example

1. In a session on introducing a new product contract:

♦ Assign one team Product Details.

♦ Assign one team Exclusions.

♦ Assign one team Legal Terms.

♦ Assign one team Exceptions.

2. In a session on Company Policies:

♦ Assign one team Sexual Harassment.

♦ Assign one team Workplace Violence.

♦ Assign one team Attendance and Time-Off Policies.

♦ Assign one team Business Ethics.

Content to Support Active Learning

Communication

We've all been communicating since we were born. With all that practice, we should be good. Right? Right. In fact, all of us can improve our communication skills. Communication is the key to success, whether between employees, customers and suppliers, parents and children, or any of a dozen relationships. Every individual and organization would be more successful by improving communication.

This section offers content ideas for training the one skill that most of us still need to work on. Activities introduce the importance of stories and words in communication and expand our awareness and address the challenges we all face.

33   Communication Challenges

Overview

> Help participants understand the power of two-way conversation and true dialogue with this communications skills reinforcement.

Participants

Any number and anyone can do this activity.

Procedure

1. Have participants pair up, preferably with someone they don't know well, and sit back to back. If there is an odd number, you can have a group of three with two drawing and one person giving directions.

2. Give each participant who will be giving directions a printed picture of a simple household item. Things like an iron, a microwave, a vacuum, a fan, a blender, a scale, and so on. Use simple stick type drawings versus pictures. These are easy to find on the web.

3. The person giving directions can only describe the item using graphic shapes, symbols, and sizes. They may not give the purpose or name of the item. They cannot ask questions of the drawer and the drawer cannot ask questions of the person giving directions. The person giving directions may not look at the drawing during the strategy.

4. When the drawer feels they know what the picture is, only then they can then ask, "Is it a _____?"

Debrief

Ask questions and facilitate discussion using the following as starting ideas:

- How difficult was it as the person giving directions to only use shapes, symbols, and sizes?

Contributed by Pam Nintrup, Project and Process Professionals

- How difficult was it as the drawer to not be able to ask questions?
- How did you (both parties) feel as the strategy proceeded?

Variations

1. Use pictures related to a specific topic, for example, company products, sports, or tools.

2. Switch places and complete a second round prior to the debriefing so both parties experience the strategy equally.

Case Example

In a sales workshop, you could use company products and then ask questions like:

- How can you more clearly explain this product to a customer?
- How can you use this information to work with marketing on better sales materials?
- What did you learn about communications that will help you with your customer interaction?

34 Generational Communication Awareness

Overview

This is a strategy to develop greater awareness of the differences in communication styles, language, and tools among the generations.

Participants

No number limitations, but requires representation of three or four generations who have working relationships, for example, project teams in departments with staff at all levels.

Procedures

1. State that the ability to exchange ideas, knowledge, support, and advice is essential for the development of trust and respect. Communication—the understanding, acceptance, and appreciation for the various methods and tools that enable people to express their thoughts—is essential to successful intergenerational relationships. By the end of this activity you will be more cognizant that people need to be "on the same communication wavelength" for a multigenerational workforce to establish an environment with high levels of engagement, performance, and productivity.

2. Have participants form small groups across the generations to discuss the ways in which they communicate most frequently and comfortably.

3. Provide each group with paper and ask them to identify a recorder/reporter. Ask them to take 15 minutes to discuss the following:

   ◆ What are the two ways of communication that you use most frequently and why?

   ◆ What do you think of the ways of communication that other people use?

Contributed by Annabelle Reitman, EdD, Career Management Strategist

◆ How do you think attitudes/mindsets about different communication styles can impact effective work relationships across the generations?

4. When time is up, ask the reporter to give a brief summary of outcomes of discussion to the group at large.

5. Ask which communication skills, tools, or techniques they would like to improve to develop better working relationships with colleagues from different generations.

Debrief

• How have your overall perceptions about other generations changed or been altered?

• What characteristics have you learned regarding other generations' ways of communicating?

• What one new communication method, tool, or way will you integrate into the way you communicate?

• How will you apply this knowledge on your job?

Variations

This learning strategy can be adapted for initiating new employee services, for example, mentoring programs, managers as coaches, as well as for leadership development training.

Case Example

The original intergenerational communication learning strategy was used in the Mentoring Partnership Model pilot program with the ATD DC Chapter. Mentoring partnerships were formed across the generations. The results of the discussion were evident in the partnership learning agreements that were established. A variety of communication methods and tools were included and used.

35   Tell It in a Story

Overview

Use this strategy to reinforce the belief in participants that they can tell interesting and captivating stories. It supports learning events for developing storytelling skills in leaders and others needing to inspire followers.

Participants

Unlimited; participants work in pairs or triads

Procedure

1. Divide the group into two-person discussion teams.

2. Ask participants to share life events that involved fire or water with their teammates.

3. Provide one minute so they can organize their thoughts and three minutes to tell the stories.

4. After completing the first life event, switch roles and repeat.

5. After completing the second round, ask the teammates to share with each other their impression of the story. You may wish to have these questions on a slide or flipchart page.

   ◆ What made the story interesting?

   ◆ How believable was the storyteller?

   ◆ How would you describe the emotion from the storyteller?

   ◆ How did the storyteller draw you into the story and the outcome?

   ◆ What other aspects of the story did you notice?

_____

Contributed by Kenneth Stein, EdD, CPLP, SPHR, Successful Endeavors

Debrief

- Ask participants how many think they are storytellers. Usually very few will raise their hands.

- Ask participants to share their reaction to the shared stories.

- Ask for volunteers to share the story they told to their partner. Ask who would like to nominate their partners to share their stories (be careful to ensure no pressure is felt).

- Ask for feedback on what participants learned about the innate ability to tell stories.

- Tie participants' comments to key storytelling characteristics as the learning event progresses.

Variations

1. Divide the group into triads. Ask the third person to report their impression of the speakers to the triad; after the end of both rounds ask the observer to provide feedback about how animated they were, how interesting the story was, how much emotion they felt, whether the story held your interest, and other things they may have noticed. Then have each speaker share personal reactions with each other or have the third person tell a story within the group.

2. Ask the group to complete this exercise over a lunch or extended break and report out upon return.

Case Example

In a session for leaders to learn to use storytelling as a leadership tool:

- Open with examples of inspirational leadership storytelling. You could show video clips or have individuals read short stories from known leaders.

- Ask participants to share their memories of inspirational stories they heard from leaders. Ask the group to define the point of the story and what made it so memorable.

36	It's In the Words

Overview

Use the learning strategy to have participants experience a creative way to define and communicate customer service and ultimately to raise the service bar.

Participants

15 to 25 people in five small groups in a typical learning session

Procedure

1. Prepare a collection of 5 to 10 keywords associated with service excellence. For example, you may have words like "Delight," "Surprise," "Grandmother," "Extraordinary," "Wholeheartedly," "Beyond," "Extra mile," "Listen," "Engage," "Interest," and "Sincere."

2. Have the keywords printed in a big font size using Comic Sans size 72. Prepare five envelopes containing the same set of words.

3. Begin the activity by asking each group to define "customer service" in their own words, to be written on a flipchart page. Give the groups five minutes to develop their own definition.

4. Give each group an envelope containing the set of keywords. Tell the participants to use the keywords in the envelope to enhance their original definition for customer service. They have 10 minutes to incorporate at least two keywords. The definitions are to be in complete sentences created as a group, *not* individually.

5. Each definition must contain at least two of the key words, and when ready, tell them they should write the new customer service definitions on a flipchart page.

6. After 10 minutes each of the groups display and share their original definition of customer service and the keyword-assisted service definition.

Contributed by Peter Cheng, PhD, PACE OD Consulting Pte Ltd Singapore

Debrief

- What key difference(s) do you see between the first customer service definitions and those that are keyword-assisted?
- What does it suggest about the impact communication can have on customer service?
- What will you do differently in the future to extend service excellence to your customers?

Variation

1. You may ask the participants to incorporate at least three or four keywords in their definition. In this case you may want to give them up to eight keywords so they have a larger selection.
2. You may wish to laminate the words so you can reuse them.
3. You may wish to give each team a different set of words.

Case Example

This activity has been used for training both new and existing internal staff, to challenge their paradigm in the way they communicate with customers. It can be used when a team leader or manager wants to increase the service standards to differentiate from their competitors.

Diversity and Inclusion

Whether you are working in the international arena where you need to understand cultural assumptions or working domestically in an environment that is becoming more culturally diverse, it is certain that this topic is on your "required list." Even if we know the importance of diversity and inclusion, we still may struggle with presenting it in a learning session. These activities will impact your learners from "hello" to exploring how we may be limiting ourselves.

37   Cultural Limitations in Clay

Overview

This learning strategy creates pathways toward effective communication and helps to eliminate potential barriers among people of diverse cultures and backgrounds. It promotes teamwork and an understanding of and appreciation for cross-cultural diversity.

Participants

6 to 16 in most learning situations

Procedure

1. Explain that the self-imposed limitations we accumulate throughout our interactions with others, through media, geography, or other method might have a bearing on how we perceive others. Cultural limitations are the lens (worldview) through which we interact with others based on our own perceptions. These are not stereotypes or prejudices since they are formulated based on how comfortable we are within our own identities.

2. Ask participants to gather in a circle and give each participant the same size piece of different colored clay so that no two participants have the same color.

3. Tell participants to mingle around the room interacting with each other. Explain that they may choose to have conversations with someone else or within small groups. Each participant may either choose to give a piece of their clay to the person they meet, or they can choose to withhold from sharing a piece of their clay, depending on their comfort level. Add that there is no right or wrong to this exercise as it serves also as a strategy for greater cultural awareness and self-awareness.

Contributed by Aurora Brito, Teachers College Columbia University and Annette Pröeschold, consultant

4. Allow about 10 minutes for this process. Then ask everyone to gather around again.

5. Explain that the exercise is about conscious choice and comfort level of interaction with others. One can choose to gravitate toward others who are similar in terms of position, industry, physical attributes, and cultural affiliations or to bridge differences.

Debrief

- Analyze your piece of clay. Does it look like a little globe with various colors? How many have no clay left?

- How comfortable were you in moving about the room and talking with others?

- With whom did you share pieces of your clay and what motivated you to do so?

- With whom did you not share pieces of your clay and what prevented you from doing so?

- What emotions came up for you during this exercise?

- Are you extroverted or introverted? Were you afraid to interact with those who may be different?

- If you have no clay left, your worldview, ability to interact with others, and your self-concept probably enables you to share parts of yourself with ease in various settings (work or school, for example). In this case, you gave away pieces of yourself and this is evidence that you mingled with others and left a bit of yourself behind with them.

- How many colors did you receive from others? If there are only a few swatches of colors (maybe less than four), your worldview and comfort level may enable you to interact with only a few people at any one time in a given setting.

- What did you learn about yourself? About others?

- What did you learn about bridging differences? How will you take what you learned into your work and into the world?

Variations

1. You can wander around and silently observe participants.

2. An alternative way to conduct the exercise is to have the participants allow the other people with whom they are interacting take a piece of their clay. There is an openness and vulnerability in allowing another to choose you by taking a piece of your clay. This deviation shows how others are likely or unlikely to want to know us based on their own cultural limitations. If the one you interact with feels comfortable with you, they may ask to take a piece of your clay, evidence that despite your comfort level, you are engaging and authentic in the interaction.

Case Examples

These are questions to ask when practicing team building, diversity awareness, and cross-cultural understanding in a higher education or cohort program setting:

- How much of your comfort level are you willing to stretch to bridge differences with others who are not the same as you?

- What can you do to increase a greater understanding of the similarities between other cohort members or classmates of different backgrounds, socio-economic backgrounds, and race and ethnic and gender/sexual orientation/religious affiliations?

- What can you do to become more consciously aware of cultural differences without judgment or personal cultural limitations?

38   Celebrate Differences

Overview

Use this activity to demonstrate that even those who are different from us have more in common with us. It can be adapted to online with a chatroom.

Participants

15 to 30 participants

Procedure

1. Ask participants to find someone in the group who is the most unlike you and identify four ways you are different in four minutes.

2. After four minutes, ask the pairs to identify four ways they are the same. Add that "same" should have a bit more depth and specificity than "we are both women" or "we both like to eat." They have four minutes for this task.

3. After four minutes, have each pair join with another pair to find four ways they are all the same. They have four minutes.

4. After four minutes, have each quad join with another quad to find four ways that all eight individuals are the same. They have six minutes.

5. Stop the exercise and ask for a few examples. Move to the debrief.

Debrief

- What did you expect when we started this activity?

- In the first round, was it easier to determine how you were different or how you were the same? Why do you suppose that was?

- Why do we get so caught up in similarities and differences?

- What difference has this activity made in how you will approach others in the future?

Variations

1. If you are short of time you could stop after the quads' discussion. If you have more time and a large group you could take the activity to the next level with 16 participants.

2. You could offer prizes for most creative similarities.

3. This is a good activity to kick off a diversity workshop.

Case Example

A 22-member public affairs team had few disagreements and issues, but their work was divided and their travel schedule was such that it was difficult for them to get to know each other or what each group did on the team. The team combined all 22 for the finale and found many things they all had in common.

39   Connecting through Hello

Overview

Use this activity to open any learning session, but especially if it focuses on relationships. Building on a "hello" activity by asking the connecting question of "how are you as a person on earth today" helps participants understand how to support each other or celebrate enhancing the sense of community.

Participants

This process can and has been used with very small groups (in both a training setting as well as team meetings in day-to-day work flow) and in groups as large as 2,000 people.

Procedure

1. Begin by discussing community at work. People are social beings and, in a workplace context, they need to feel safe and included if they are to speak up, have critical conversations, and do their best work. Many people would say they don't feel safe or welcome to contribute or included in their team if no one speaks to them. If you are going to have a meeting in which people feel safe to speak up, saying hello is a good way for people to begin to feel included, seen, and connected to others. A simple act of greeting tells others "I see you" and leads to people feeling as if their presence (and contributions) will matter.

2. Have people stand in a circle, leaving their hands free of items. Explain the purpose and process. The following is a script that has been effective:

   ◆ We are going to be involved in an easy activity that addresses one of the most important issues in organizations today—creating an inclusive work environment.

   ◆ You can't have a community of effort if people don't say hello.

Contributed by Frederick A. Miller and Judith H. Katz, The Kaleel Jamison Consulting Group, Inc.

◆ People are often more motivated to get to their email than to say "hello" to the people they see along the way. People on work teams often go directly to task instead of greeting all the members of the team first.

◆ In many places, people who are new to the organization or different from others get the fewest "hellos."

3. Say that we are all going to greet each other. Add that a greeting can take many forms:

◆ Make eye contact and give a culturally appropriate greeting.

◆ This isn't a hugging process! Greet others in a way in which you feel comfortable—and in a way that is comfortable for the other person. If you aren't clear about what that is, ask!

◆ If you don't feel well or you don't want to make any physical contact, a "fist bump" or wave is fine.

4. Reform the standing circle. Prompt people to look around the circle to ensure they have greeted each person and take a moment to say hello to anyone whom they missed.

5. After a few moments of informal silence to allow participants to refocus their attention from individual interaction to the group setting, ask each person to reflect on the question "How are you doing as a person on earth on a zero to 10 scale—zero being I am not doing well at all, 10 being I am fabulous?" Ask for a volunteer to start the response process and go around the circle so that each person shares her or his number.

6. Once everyone has responded, ask those with low and high numbers if they would like to share more about their response. If time allows, you could have all partici-pants share the meaning of their number. By asking this question it provides more insight into how people are entering a meeting or education session, and group members can be more responsive to other team members' needs.

Debrief

• How did you feel about saying hello to everyone? What was the impact?

• Do you say hello to your colleagues each day? If you do, great! If you don't, do you think it would make a difference?

- In what ways might knowing your colleagues' "numbers"—how they are feeling on a daily basis—change or strengthen your interactions with them?

Variations

1. Hellos: In very large groups (50+) where it isn't possible to greet each person in a short period of time, set a time boundary with the instruction, "Greet as many people as you can in ___ minutes."

2. Some facilitator comments that might be helpful or needed to frame the "person on earth" portion of the exercise:

   ◆ The process of having people share their number is about having people feel heard and joined/supported, not judged.

   ◆ Where a person is ("their number") is a point in time and can change—sometimes dramatically—during the course of a day.

   ◆ Having people share where they are and the reason for their "number" helps people keep people from assuming a person's energy, mood, or affect is about them and allows them to consider how to interact with that person in a productive way.

Case Examples

1. As is often the case, in a recent education session for managers, after participants greeted each other, one manager shared that he recognized some of the names of other managers from the invitation, had never had an opportunity to interact with some of them, and had never really greeted or "met" some others, even though they sometimes attended the same meetings. The activity enabled him to quickly connect names and faces and feel he had many points of commonality with other attendees.

2. In a session where people were able to share how they were as a person on earth, the conversation that resulted gave the group insight into a colleague's struggle with a sick parent. Knowing this was impacting her allowed others to see her quietness and lower energy from a more informed perspective.

Leadership

Leadership is the number one need in most organizations and probably has had more books and articles published about it than any other topic. Leadership is studied from a business, military, and personal perspective. And authors debate whether leadership is a science, an art, or a bit of both. This section addresses a topic plaguing most organizations with a shortage of prepared leaders for the future. The activities suggest ideas to develop skills for leaders at all levels and offer a mix of skills and reflection.

40   Listening to Collaboration

Overview

This exercise introduces the concepts of leadership, collaboration, and "leader-less" groups. It's an effective way to get a new cohort of learners to begin collaborating and thinking outside the frame of their own immediate challenges and situations.

Participants

Up to 15 learners who are either experienced or prospective leaders and who want to become more capable of understanding nuances of collaboration

Procedure

1. Secure the participation of a small musical ensemble, ideally a string quartet or jazz group. These musicians will be ready to play various versions of some of their repertoire, demonstrate improvisational skills, and talk about how they play without a formal conductor, each assuming various leadership roles during rehearsals and performances.

2. Without preparing the learners, take them to a place where the musical group has assembled and introduce them to the musicians. Tell the learners that this will provide both a break and an opportunity to talk about some concepts related to the class. Have the musicians play a short piece.

3. Ask the learners, "Who was the conductor?" Ask the musicians to describe how they follow each other and how the performance of the piece is led. This process can be enhanced through various performances of a short musical section where the musicians demonstrate typical team problems such as one member carrying the entire workload, one person being on a "different page," everyone vying for control, and so on. Ask the learners what they heard and observed.

Contributed by Diane Gayeski, PhD, Roy H. Park School of Communications, Ithaca

4. Based on previous experiences with teams, the learners can request to see and hear various scenarios that they have encountered. Improvisation could be utilized to demonstrate the organic nature of working on a team. The musicians might also suggest other variations and discussion topics from their own experiences (both good and bad).

Debrief

- To the learners: How does working as a musical ensemble relate to the work you do?

- To the musicians: How does leadership work within the ensemble? How did you develop as an ensemble? What's it like to introduce a new member? What makes a great ensemble? How does a performer lead/follow, perform as an individual/as a group, control/be in a non-controlling state—even at the same time?

- In music, there are formal genres (for instance, classical music performed with a score and conductor) and "in the moment" genres (for instance, jazz and improvisation). How does the leadership vary? How does this apply to different kinds of organizations or business settings or individual circumstances? What happens when there is an absence of a score and a lack of a plan in the moment? Are there links to complexity? Can complexity be demonstrated in the musical demonstrations?

Variations

1. A similar exercise might be done by watching a football team practice and observing the various leaders (coach, assistant coaches, quarterback).

2. It's also ideal as a surprise or break from traditional classroom activities.

3. It is especially appropriate for those who will be leading creative and innovative groups.

Case Example

In a graduate course session for mid-level managers in the media industry who aspire to be leaders of innovation, we hired a string quartet that had worked together for several years. They were able to play a number of variations of the same piece—for example, with one leader, with two people vying for leadership, with nobody leading, and other situations. The instructor prompted the learners to pay close attention to body language and cues. An interesting discussion followed, as the learners asked the quartet about their previous experiences in musical groups and which ones "clicked" and which ones did not. An additional topic was the impact of the audience and how that dynamic changes the experiences and performance of the musicians.

All of this was brought back to various concepts of leadership that had been discussed previously—the differences among leadership, authority, charisma, and responsibility—and the ways that leaders influence those around them. This led to many examples brought up by the learners, and to ideas about how to effectively lead groups, especially artistic and creative individuals.

Note: This approach was designed by Carrie Reuning-Hummel who designed and executed the exercise described in the case and has offered versions of this for various training engagements. The course was co-taught by Professor Gordon Rowland and Dean Diane Gayeski.

41 Focus a Discussion

Overview

Use this to focus discussion on the future to develop vision statements or the present to develop mission statements. This method encourages participation and engages all members. It can be used in a variety of settings to encourage those who generally do not speak up or contribute openly.

Participants

Key decision makers, a group no larger than 50, but this can be done in a very large group with results consolidated and then voted on.

Procedure

1. Explain the purpose of the activity: If creating a vision statement, define what that is (the entity's future desired state within three to five years); if creating a mission statement, define what that is (what the entity does—its purpose). Provide examples. For other topics (new programs, new services, learning objectives, creative content), have an example of what the topic is so all understand the end outcome.

2. Divide participants into groups of no more than five (no smaller than two) and have each member in the group generate a list of words that signify what each person thinks are the most important things for the entity to be doing in the future (if doing a vision statement) or to be known for (if doing a mission statement). They should do this individually, silently writing down the words on a sheet of paper. Encourage them to generate at least five words. Give them about 10 minutes to do this.

Contributed by Patricia L. Johnson PhD; Certified Health and Wellness Coach, St. Luke's Health System

3. Have all participants share their words and discuss why they chose the words they did.

4. Have the group pick the top three words from their group that all can agree on.

5. Each group reports out to the facilitator, who transcribes the words using a laptop and projector using Word or some other document software package so all can see. Even repeated words are added to the list. It is important that everyone's top picks are shown.

6. Invite clarifications to the words—what was intended by the word, how that particular word became the top pick.

7. Invite the group to eliminate duplications. It is important that the group do this, not you. You will generally end up with about 10 to 12 words.

8. Using the remaining words, have the groups get back together and have them individually construct sentences using all the words. Ask them to share their sentences with their small group and as a group select the one that they agree on.

9. Using the laptop and projector, transcribe the various statements. Read them aloud to the group.

10. Ask if there are one or two that sentences the group are most excited about. Move those to the top of your document. Ask for clarifications, changes, or edits. At this point the group will generally move toward making a decision on one statement, incorporating key words or phrases that are important to the group. Tell the group they have written a draft. Email it to one or two members of the group.

11. Have them review the statement(s) at their next meeting to confirm that it meets their needs.

Debrief

- How did this process contribute to your understanding of each other's perspectives?

- Did everyone participate fully? To what do you attribute that?

- How did the process help you to better engage in more meaningful dialogue about the future or the present as it relates to the organization?

Variations

1. This process can be used for decision making, developing creative content, determining learning objectives, and so on.

2. If a laptop and projector are not available, a flipchart can be used to capture the words and statements. It takes longer.

3. Another option is to provide learners with half sheets of colored unlined paper and markers on which they can write their words. You can collect and post them. (Use flipchart paper sprayed with spray mount glue). Depending on the size of the group, this can be very useful or very complicated. Then follow the same process for eliminating duplicate words, clarifying word choices, and so on. Follow the same process for sentence construction but write the sentences on the flipcharts or a whiteboard if available.

4. When developing new services or programs, rather than words, the participants could be asked to develop lists of programs or services and follow the process to construct a list of top 3, 5, or 10 services or programs, and so on.

Case Examples

1. A small group of physicians in a practice group wrote a mission statement.

2. A large group of board members for a not-for-profit business wrote a vision statement.

3. A large group of members of an arts council developed a list of new programs.

42   Best Boss

Overview

Use this strategy to get participants to discuss the importance of quality interpersonal skills in a physical or virtual classroom.

Participants

One to hundreds of managers/supervisors or individual contributors who may be promoted to leadership roles

Procedure

1. Ask participants to think of their Best Boss (or bosses) and to identify the behaviors, traits, and characteristics displayed that makes them want to label the person "best."

2. Have them write the four to five traits they most value, and prioritize them, labeling #1 as most valued and so forth.

3. Ask participants to share their "#1s" while you list them on flipchart or whiteboard (physical or virtual).

Debrief

- Ask participants how they feel when working with or for a person who displays these traits. Specific answers may vary, but most answers lead to feeling valued, feeling that what they do/how they are spending their time makes a difference/an impact/is important. Write responses on a flipchart or whiteboard (physical or virtual).

- Ask participants how feeling this way, for example, valued, impacts their work. Specific answers may vary, but most answers lead to the impact of working harder,

Contributed by Lynne Lazaroff, M.S, The Leadership Dimension

working better, more productivity, better quality, and greater innovation and learning.

- Ask participants whether a majority of the traits listed are technical skills or interpersonal skills.

- The lists are always 90–100% interpersonal skills, allowing the participants to make the point themselves of the value of interpersonal skills. Never say that technical skills are not important, just that interpersonal skills are as important, because they have at least as much impact on quality, quantity, and innovation and learning as technical skills.

Variations

1. Best Colleague
2. Best Leader
3. Best Team Member

Case Example

Examples of traits, whether asking about bosses/team leaders or colleagues/team members, include honest, consistent, keep me informed, provide opportunities to learn/develop, provide feedback (positive and constructive), admit when they make mistakes, have a sense of humor, treat me/get to know me as an individual, and ask for my ideas/help/input.

43   Learning through Dialogue

Overview

Based on the Appreciative Inquiry (AI) approach conceptualized by David Coop-errider, this strategy can be used to inculcate team leadership skills in middle level managers, while promoting self-reflection and collaborative learning.

Participants

12 to 20 middle level managers having more than two years of experience sitting at tables arranged in a circular format so participants can have face-to-face conversations

Procedure

1. Introduce the topic (team leadership) to the participants. List topic-related questions on a flip chart/PPT slide/whiteboard/in participant's materials. See the case example for questions.

2. Divide the group into dyads. Ask each dyad to converse using the question list. Also ask all participants to write down their partners' comments on the blank paper provided to them. Encourage them to probe their partners to reveal the maximum information. Ensure that all the participants play the role of an interviewer as well as interviewee.

3. After the conversation ask each dyad to join another dyad thus forming a group of four. Members will share their notes with the other members of the group. A group leader will prepare a consolidated list of the input from all the members. Ask this person to present it to the larger group. Write the points from each subgroup on the board or flipchart.

4. Ask each participant to draw an image of an ideal team leader taking into consideration the attributes, competencies, and behavior based on the discussion. Ask them to share the images with the entire group.

Contributed by Mitu Mandal, Educational Consultant, India limited, India

5. Ask members to rate themselves on a five-point scale as an ideal team leader. Encourage them to analyze how far they deviate from being an ideal team leader, what are the causes, and how can they be an ideal team leader. Ask each participant to design an action plan and share it with group members. Any of the participants can describe the action plan to the entire group.

Debrief

- How did you feel as an interviewer and as an interviewee? What happened when you shared your ideas with your partner?
- Did the exercise help you to learn about team leadership? How?
- How are you going to use this exercise in your organization?

Variation

If you are short of time, steps two and three can be combined eliminating the dyadic conversation, and moving directly to the small groups. In this case ensure that each member discusses his or her experiences while other members probe.

Case Example

These questions provided direction to the participants for conversations. The participants can include additional questions. An effort is made to identify the positives, the best things, the success, and the qualities of the individual, which is the basic premise of the Appreciative Inquiry approach.

1. Describe a person whom you consider as the best team leader.
2. What makes someone rate as the best?
3. What unique qualities, competencies, or behaviors define a great leader?
4. Can you describe a memorable event with your team leader that has inspired you?

5. What communication and decision-making styles are used by great leaders? Describe an event.

6. Apart from his/her professional image, how would you describe a great leader as a person?

7. What qualities would you like to inherit from him/her. What did you learn from him/her?

44   Brand Boosters

Overview

> This learning activity is highly flexible. It's been used for leadership development, sales teams, call centers, and frontline employees. Put simply, to improve your brand or organizational culture, look at other companies and see how you can borrow or adapt strategies in ways that matter.

Participants

This works best with participants in an intact work team, same department, shared experience or focus, or a single cohort (all call center employees or all managers, for example).

Minimum size of 10 and maximum size of 70

Procedure

1. Pre-work: Instruct participants to bring an 8x10 copy of two to three logos of companies they admire and personally rely on. These companies can be from inside or outside of the participants' industry.

2. Open the activity by saying, "Mark Twain said, 'There is no such thing as a new idea. It is impossible. We simply take a lot of old ideas and put them into a sort of mental kaleidoscope. We give them a turn and they make new and curious combinations. We keep on turning and making new combinations indefinitely; but they are the same old pieces of colored glass that have been in use through all the ages.'"

3. Ask participants to get out their logos.

4. Assign participants to groups of three with others they don't know well. Ask them to share their top three companies and logos and how they selected the companies. Encourage them to explain how they tell/share those experiences with

Contributed by Amy S. Tolbert, PhD, CSP, ECCO International

others: Do you use Facebook? Twitter? Blogs? Email? Casual conversation? Ask each participant to relay a personal story as to why they choose to do business with one of the companies.

5. After 8–10 minutes, ask participants to reconvene.

6. Bring the group together and have all participants post their three logos on the wall or on flipchart pages you have posted.

7. Open a discussion with these questions:

   ◆ What trends did you notice in other participants' choice of companies? (post on a flipchart)

   ◆ What did you notice about the company logos that everyone brought to the training? (post on a flipchart)

   ◆ Elicit a few stories; ask for a few participants to share their story and experience with a company

   ◆ What trends emerged? (post on a flipchart)

   ◆ Recap lists from the flipchart, emphasizing your training topic/theme message.

Debrief

- What do these companies do really well?
- What can we borrow from these companies?
- How can we apply the culture/model of the admired companies to our organization?

Variations

1. Discuss as one large group.

2. Break the group into small groups and give each group one admired company and two questions to answer:

   ◆ What is the key attribute we admire about this company?

   ◆ How can we apply that attribute to our company?

3. Take one of your company's strategic objectives (increase market share, develop new products faster, improve customer service) and apply the admired companies to that strategic objective.

Case Examples

1. In a leadership development meeting you could ask these questions:

◆ How is an admired company's culture different than ours? What could we change?

◆ How do we view an admired company's employees? What can we, as leaders, do to promote that same attribute?

◆ Consumers are in charge, just like our clients or customers! Like Walt Disney said, "Do what you do so well that they will want to see it again and bring their friends." Control is moving away from the companies that produce goods and services and toward the people who buy them. Consumers have demonstrated that they understand marketing; they feel smart and capable and will search out information, products, and services they value. Even in a tough economy, consumers are holding onto that control. Personal empowerment isn't just what consumers want; it's what they expect, in all domains.

◆ This exercise highlighted the fact that we're all consumers and that we patronize companies because of their service, attention to detail, ease of purchase, convenience, reliability, how they make us feel, and so on. No different than our industry and our partners, patients, clients, and customers.

2. In a meeting of salespeople you could ask these questions:

◆ What is your first impression of the salespeople of the admired company? Do we do that? If we don't, how can we change?

◆ What is your lasting impression of the salespeople of the admired company? Would you provide a referral?

◆ If you've ever had a problem with a product or service, how did you react? Was it fixed? Did they "save" you as a customer? What could you do, that they do?

45   Touchpoint

_____ **Overview** _____

This lively activity sets the stage to discuss how a team's work flow affects service effectiveness and efficiency.

Participants

All levels of participants are suitable

Procedure

1. Ask everyone to form a circle.

2. Say that everyone will have an opportunity to throw and receive the tennis ball once in each round. Only the leader will be the first to throw and the last to receive to signify that the item has been circulated through all the hands of all participants. The throwing must be done across at least two other people.

3. The leader begins with the first toss. Each person who throws must first call out the name of the participant who will receive it. The item is thrown and received by everyone in the circle and returns to the leader to receive it. The goal is to keep the ball from dropping.

4. Appoint a leader to start and end the activity. Give the leader a tennis ball and ask the leader to toss it to someone. Continue as described.

5. The first round of the activity establishes the pattern of throwers and recipients within the circle. This pattern of who throws to whom will be repeated in subsequent rounds.

6. The activity will start with one ball first. After the team has completed this at least two times, begin to increase the number of balls to raise the challenge. Add one ball at round three, then another at round five, and so forth.

7. The goal of no dropped balls represents no dropped tasks at work while serving the customer as a team.

Contributed by Lily Cheng, PhD, PACE OD Consulting Pte Ltd. Singapore

Debrief

- Reflecting upon the activity, how would you rate your team's effectiveness and efficiency in accomplishing the task, within the given rules? Why?
- What were the effective and efficient behaviors you observed?
- How does individual effectiveness and efficiency impact team and organizational performance?
- What process in the workplace is similar to this activity? Which elements are similar?
- What can we do to increase our team's effectiveness and efficiency?

Variations

1. You can use other items such as balloons, toys, beanbags, wadded up paper, or apples. Add various items instead of all one kind.
2. Lead a discussion about the importance of team service excellence. Ask, How can we give each other the support needed to have no dropped balls?
3. A variation of the activity could also address the importance of peer coaching at work when one or two team members lack the competency to perform tasks well, impacting the team's overall performance.

Case Example

The activity is effective with intact teams, where existing and new members need to work closely together. In situations where there are changes in the workflow among teams or across teams in an organization, this is an excellent activity for working teams to appreciate and understand the importance of effective working relationships.

Teamwork and Team Building

Successful teams are an asset few organizations can afford to be without. Workplaces have been focused on teamwork for half of a century, yet we are still learning how to be good team players, how to build teams, how to support teams, how to lead teams, and how to reward teams. No matter what your job, you are most likely engaged in working with teams in one way or another. Many of us in the training and consulting professions are intimately involved in teamwork. This section provides a nice mix of skill development, knowledge of teamwork, and building a team when things are not working as well as they could.

46 Crest of Teams

Overview

This process aligns team members by presenting and hearing the insight of each team member. It can work in any physical setting but is more difficult in a virtual setting.

Participants

Members of a new team; or members of an old team that need to work better together

Procedure

1. Give each participant a flipchart sheet (or large poster board) with a large crest already drawn on the chart and divided into six sections.

2. Have participants take 10 minutes to fill in the space on the crest the answers to the following six questions:

   ♦ What is a personal value you hold dear (fairness, freedom, excellence)?

   ♦ What is your most prized inanimate physical object? Or, if your house was on fire and you got all your family and pets out and could go back for one item, what would it be?

   ♦ How do you typically help a team?

   ♦ How do you typically hinder a team?

   ♦ If you were to describe this team as a mode of transportation, what would you select (a jet plane, a bus filled with teenagers, farm tractor)?

   ♦ What part do you play in the mode of transportation you selected? (I am the wing, the engine, the sail.)

3. Have each participant present his or her shield without interruption and taking questions only for clarification.

4. Have the team react to each person's choices on his or her crest after the presentation.

5. Debrief after all have finished their crest presentations.

Contributed by Chip R. Bell, Chip Bell Group

Debrief

- What answers were most in common; most different? So what are the implications?
- What were the surprises?
- If you were a renowned team counselor hearing these answers, what cautions would you provide this team? What advice would you offer?
- How will you deal with individual team members differently based on what you just learned?

Variations

1. Following all presentations, have the team establish some initial agreements about how they plan to work together.

2. Have participants draw their six answers instead of using words.

3. Have people contract with specific team members regarding ways they will call on their strengths and/or give them feedback about ways they hinder effective teamwork when observed.

4. Use an audience response system to have people register reactions to a preplanned set of binary questions about the crests and what they learned.

Case Example

This was used with the executive leadership of a major bank in Central America as a way to start a two-day team alignment retreat. It became a foundation for the rest of the session. People immediately gained insight into each other and began contracting and creating important team agreements. This is more than an icebreaker. Done correctly it can be foundational for a class on teamwork or a team-building experience. For example, one person had a very strong value around honesty. He became an important "conscience" of the team and was granted permission to call any team member out when he believed they were not being completely honest and frank in their interaction. As he carried out his assigned role, others gained confidence in being open and candid with each other.

47 Wall of Reality and Greatness

Overview

Use this activity with groups or leaders to establish an aligned current state on a strategy, and to have an honest conversation about where the disconnects and improvement opportunities are within the function or across the business.

Participants

5 to 50 with enough room for movement

Procedure

1. Review what's going on in the organization that is affecting your team today. This could be a strategic initiative, change, or challenge the company faces.

2. Tell the group that every organization has both strengths and barriers to executing strategy, and this is an opportunity to examine both aspects of this team/group.

3. Give everyone three to five large-sized sticky notes. Using one note per thought, ask them to write those cultural, behavioral, or strategic "Truth Statements" about the organization that are leading to canyons within the organization. When they are done, ask them to stick their notes on a blank portion of a wall. As they are placing the notes, ask them to attempt to group them with other notes they think are similar.

4. Ask the group to write down those attributes that allow the organization to be successful and contribute to the execution of strategy. When they are done, ask them to stick their notes on a blank portion of a wall, grouping them into common themes. Play a leading role in the affinity grouping process.

5. Gather the team around the sticky notes and ask them to read all of the notes aloud and to share their observations. You can do this for both the strengths and barriers sections.

6. Ask the group: "As you look at these Truth Statements, how have you personally contributed to them? How have you benefited?" Encourage all team members to participate. Thank them for their candor.

Contributed by Rich Berens, Root Inc.

7. Ask the group to vote on the top three Truth Statements they believe the team should tackle directly and immediately. They can use check marks, stickers, or small sticky notes to place their votes.

8. Count the votes and announce the top three issues.

Debrief

- Be sure to spend a good amount of time discussing the questions outlined in process step six. It is critical that you don't rush through these questions; let them soak in with the team.

- Engage your group in an action-planning brainstorm to address the issues and the top Truth Statements identified:

  ◆ What is the desired result?

  ◆ How will we measure success?

  ◆ Who needs to be involved in removing this barrier/solving this problem?

  ◆ To make this happen, what changes do all of us need to commit to making?

  ◆ What's at stake if we do not succeed?

Variation

At times you might only want to focus on strengths or opportunities, rather than both.

Case Examples

1. An organization (any industry) is going through a large-scale change, and leaders need to be engaged in what aspects of their culture and behaviors they want to keep and what aspects need to change. This activity will drive honest dialogue and buy-in for the change that is needed.

2. A learning team is trying to get clear with its business partner about the outcome of a large-scale training initiative. This activity will emphasize where the business has strengths and opportunities and how to focus the learning strategy for maximum effectiveness.

48   Hit Your Numbers

Overview

This experiential activity requires team members to hit (touch) a series of numbers in order and in the fastest time to explore team process improvement.

Participants

Two teams of 6 to 10 people exploring process improvement initiatives

Procedure

1. To prepare, print numbers 1 to 60 on quarter-page size paper. Randomly lay the numbers on the floor or a table and rotate them to various positions. Circle the numbers with a boundary using tape and string, or draw with chalk. Use tape or string (or draw with chalk) two starting lines about 10 feet from the boundary on either side of the circled numbers. This becomes the playing field. Each team will stand behind its starting line. See Figure 11.1.

2. Divide participants into two groups and have each team gather behind its starting line. Share the rules of the activity:

   ◆ The numbers must be hit (touched) in sequence from lowest to highest.

   ◆ Time starts when the first person enters the playing field and you will time each trial.

   ◆ Time stops when all players exit the playing field.

   ◆ Numbers may not be moved, rearranged, or turned.

   ◆ Borderlines may not be moved.

   ◆ All team members must touch at least one number.

3. The goal is to complete this activity as quickly as possible without any quality errors.

Contributed by Dr. Tim Buividas, Corporate Learning Institute

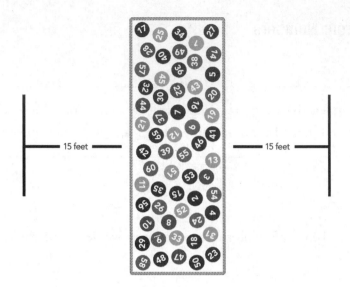

Figure 11.1

4. Tell them how much time they have to complete the activity (from 15 to 45 minutes depending upon what you are trying to accomplish). They can do as many trials as they choose. At the end of the activity time, they will run one last trial for their final score.

Debrief

- As a team, what did you do well?

- As a team, where did you struggle?

- Specifically, what did it take to continuously improve your process and work with a high delivery of results while maintaining high quality?

- If you were to do this activity again, what would you differently to increase your performance and results?

- How is this activity similar or different to how you work together now?

- What do you need to do as a team to continuously improve how you work together?

- What do you need to do to more effectively "hit your numbers" at work?

Variations

1. If numbers are touched out of sequence, you can add a five-second penalty for each one touched out of sequence.

2. You could limit the number of trials that a group has to complete the activity.

3. Start by assigning each team member three to four specific numbers to hit. Explain that it is their job to ensure that their numbers are hit. This is a play on words, and they may assume they have to hit the specific numbers which takes more time; they can only improve their time when they understand that "to ensure" can mean effectively delegating to others.

4. Have teams time their own trials.

Case Examples

1. In a manufacturing setting, you might ask: How can you improve your process to ensure that you are continuously improving your manufacturing time while increasing your quality?

2. In a sales setting, you might ask: What are best practices that you can share with each other that will help each other hit your numbers.

3. In a leadership team setting, you might ask: How can you more effectively shift your focus from a functional perspective to an organizational perspective? How can you increase alignment and support between departments and employees?

49   Who's Important?

Overview

The competitive nature of working sometimes makes employees oblivious to collaboration. This strategy makes the participants aware of their importance as well as others in achieving the goals of the team.

Participants

As many as you desire

Procedure

1. After all the participants return from lunch, ask them, "How was your lunch?"
2. Ask the participants, "Which body parts helped you at lunch?"
3. List the body parts on the flip chart/whiteboard/smartphone with a smart TV projection system.
4. Ask each participant to write a body part name from the list on a Post-it note. Collect the names. Randomly distribute the body part names and tell them to stick the Post-it note on themselves.
5. Call everybody to an open space in the center of the room/hall. Ask them to arrange themselves in a line according to the significance of the body part name they are carrying. You may need to prompt them with a question such as, "Who's most important? Which body part is most important?"

Debrief

- What criteria were used to arrange yourselves?
- Ask the person in the last position about his feeling of being the last in body part in importance. Does she/he deserve the position?

Contributed by Chandra M. Chakravartula, SAIL-DSP, India

- Ask the person in the front about his/her feeling being the first in body part hierarchy. Does she/he deserve the position?

- Ask all the participants whether there exists a way in which everybody can feel equally important by not using a linear methodology. (They should determine that forming a circle eliminates the hierarchy.)

- How does this relate to our team and the importance of its members?

- What important roles does each of you play on your team?

- What can you do as a result of this exercise to improve your ability to utilize everyone's contribution to the team?

Variation

You could use car parts. Ask participants if they were a car part what part would they be. Follow this with the same arrangement of importance.

Case Examples

1. In a team-building session, the following questions can be asked:

- What can be done about somebody in a team who feels that he/she is more important than others?

- How can somebody help a team member feel that everybody has an important role in the team?

- How everybody can work together to achieve the team goals?

2. In a leadership session one can use these questions:

- How can a leader make his team members feel important?

- What can a leader do to instill equity in the team?

- Ask a participant to share an experience when he/she felt less important due to the action of a leader.

50   Sticking Together

Overview

Use this energizing activity to reinforce brainstorming, communication, and team building. It promotes critical thinking and strategic planning, and reinforces the benefits of synergy.

Participants

5 to 10; more in small groups of 5 to 10

Procedure

1. Provide a roll of plastic wrap and a stopwatch.

2. Ask participants to stand in a group circle and squeeze really close together.

3. Ask participants on the outside edge of the group to lift their outside-facing hand above their head, except for one person (starting edge).

4. Begin wrapping the plastic wrap around the participant group by tucking the starting edge under a participant's arm, waistline height. Proceed pulling and stretching plastic wrap out of container around the group circle.

5. When you reach the starting edge participant, ask them to raise their arm. Stretch and press the plastic wrap over the starting edge. Continue to wrap two more layers of plastic wrap over the first layer, pressing down the plastic wrap as each layer is wound. Tell participants to lower their hands.

6. Mark "Start" and "Finish" lines by pointing out objects in room, or by taping a line on the floor.

7. Provide activity instructions. Tell them that this is a timed activity and the goal is that the team must move standing together from "Start" to "Finish." You will record the time it takes to complete the activity. The objective is to determine the "best" time.

Contributed by Sharon Dera, The Proficience Group, Inc.

8. Rules include that they can't break the plastic wrap. Safety is paramount: no crawling, lifting, piggy-backing. All participants' feet must remain on the floor. Ask if everyone understands the instructions. Clarify as needed.

9. Begin the activity by starting the stopwatch/timing. At the "Finish" line stop and announce the elapsed time. Ask the group if they think they can beat their first attempt.

10. Begin the activity again and the stopwatch/timing. At the "Finish" line stop and announce the elapsed time.

11. Ask the group if they think they can beat their second attempt. If they say yes, repeat the process. Announce their time. (It is good to end after three tries.)

12. Ask participants on the outside edge to each take a few steps (backward/forward as necessary), stretching the plastic wrap. The plastic wrap should stretch enough for the group to move around within the group more freely, or to actually lift the stretched ring of plastic up above their waists.

Debrief

Ask participants:

- What were some challenges you faced during the activity?
- What made it challenging? Why?
- How did you overcome the challenges?
- Were there any disagreements? If so, what were they?
- How does this relate to working as a team in your work environment?
- What are some barriers you may experience?

Variation

Conduct competition between several groups of 5 to 10 participants each.

Case Examples

- Retail store employees during a monthly store meeting

- Training department team members during staff meeting

- Group of community site managers for after-school program during staff monthly meeting

Each time the groups laugh at the beginning of the activity while being wrapped together. Then, pause and quickly try to brainstorm as the activity instructions are being given.

Most first attempts are very slow going, with the group taking small cautious steps, sometimes out of step with one another (stepping on each other's feet). When finished, this is the longest timeframe. They always want to better their time so they are eager for a second attempt.

During the second attempt, the group tries to coordinate their steps, sometimes calling out left, right, left to stay synchronized. When finished, their time is a definite improvement over the first attempt. But they are eager for a third attempt because during the first and second attempts they discover and plan new ways of improvement. During the third attempt, the group tries their coordinated steps at a faster tempo, sometimes at a quicker stride. The third attempt is always the best timing.

At the end of the activity, as the participants on the outside edge each take a few steps (backward/forward as necessary) while stretching the plastic wrap, the group suddenly realizes how they had limited themselves by not stretching their boundaries, testing the limits, or asking more questions.

The rule is: Don't break the plastic wrap. It didn't say you couldn't stretch the plastic wrap. The debrief is always beneficial, leading to comments such as:

- Be open to others point of view.

- Be willing to lead if/when necessary.

- Use critical thinking/problem solving skills to ask questions, get confirmation.

51 Team Effectiveness

--- **Overview** ---

Use this strategy to get participants to identify the skills required for organizational effectiveness and teamwork. It can also be used to introduce Lean Processes.

Participants

4 to 20 managers/supervisors and individual contributors; anyone who works in collaboration with others

Procedure

1. Collect a variety of six to eight items that are easily available: roll of masking tape, whiteboard eraser, marker, paper clip, index card, sheet of paper, name tag, ballpoint pen, packet of Post-it notes, and so on, and set them within your reach.

2. Have participants stand in a circle, while you stand just outside the circle. State that they are a start-up organization, and you are their new supervisor/manager. Lots of things are unclear, but you will provide them with information as you receive it. Let's start!

3. Ask participants to raise one hand. Explain that you will hand an object to one person, who may hand it to whomever they want, who in turn can hand it to whomever they want, and so on, till the last person hands it back to the first person.

4. As each person receives the object, they will put their hands down.

5. Say, "You must remember who gave you the object and who you gave the object to."

Contributed by Lynne Lazaroff, M.S, The Leadership Dimension

6. State the goal of the activity is that the object makes a full circuit in the same order.

7. Ask if everyone is clear on the goal/instructions? Ready for Round 1?

Round 1

No talking.

You hand the first person the object.

As the first object begins its round, hand the first person a second object, and then a third object.

Note the time it takes them to complete circuit.

State the time, and tell them that the company down the street can perform the same work in less time (if it took them 15 seconds, tell them the other company does it in 5). When they complain about the unexpected added items, remind them that things change.

Round 2

Hand an object to the same first person.

Add a new rule: Call the person's name before giving them the object.

After getting the first three objects going, add the fourth object, then the fifth through whatever number you've chosen.

Note the time it takes them to complete the circuit.

State the time; given the additional task of stating names, extra items, and the time pressure, they will have dropped items and had to pick them up, and they still will not have beat the time required.

Rounds 3, 4, 5, (or whatever number of rounds are required to beat the competition's time)

Repeat all steps with the same number of objects as in Round 2.

Hand to same person.

Call the person's name before giving them object.

Keep the sequence, complete the circuit.

Add another new rule: Objects may not hit the floor.

Also state that the overall goal is to have each person touch each object, in order.

Given that you have now clarified all of the standards/specifications (objects in same order, to same people in same order, no dropping, all must touch each object in order), they will innovate or ask if they may innovate and of course they can! Some groups may ask if they can innovate after the first round. They can! Even if they have already begun innovating, still add the extra rules at the second round.

Innovations almost always include rearranging themselves in order, and often also include having one person hold all the objects in order and have each of the others walk by them in order, touching each object, or using the masking tape to tape the objects together and passing the combined object; or having all but the first person line up in order, and having the first person hold all of the objects in order and walk quickly by all of the others, who touch the objects as they pass.

Debrief

- What happened as you conducted the activity?
  How does this activity resemble organizations?
  What happened when noise entered the system? (like rumors)
  What happened when the rules changed?

- Was there a leader?
  How did a leader evolve?
  Did the leader change? (How many times? Why? How?)

- What happened as you attempted to improve performance?
  How did you attempt improvement?
  What actions were taken? (usually, speed up)
  Was there discussion or planning?

- How many of you delivered objects to people you know?
  Why? (know the capability/competency/resource, stay safe)
  How often does that happen in your organization? (overlook new/better/different
     resources)

- If the group reorganized:
  Who initiated reorganization?
  How many attempted it, and gave up?
  What was the reaction to the reorganization?
- How often do we begin activities without knowing the true/complete goal?
- How often do we start activities without planning/thinking it through?

Variation

Instead of asking debriefing questions, mark a flipchart with two columns, and label the first with a plus and the second with a minus. Ask participants to note the actions that helped them succeed (list beneath the plus) and the actions or lack of actions that made success more difficult.

Case Example

A company had completed a merger with another larger company two months prior. The contract processing team needed to find a way to coordinate processes and to work more effectively with new colleagues. After this activity the combined team summarized a list of what they gained from the activity and what they needed to focus on to work better as a team. The list included:

- Performance improves with knowledge of true/complete goal.
- Ask questions to understand.
- Performance improves with planning.
- Use all available resources.
- Be open-minded.
- The leader sets the tone.
- We tend to connect with those we already know—branch out.
- Keep it simple.
- Be willing to share ideas, even when uncertain of outcome (with mitigation, of course).

- Be willing to try new strategies, even when you are uncertain of the outcome.
- To improve, first impulse is to speed up—a poor strategy.
- Leadership is not positional. It can be moved/shared.
- Secondary and informal leadership also exists.
- Create better, more effective teams with inclusion than with exclusion.

52   Balancing Responsibilities

Overview

Participation from all members is critical to reach a successful outcome. Use this activity to show the impact that each individual has in the overall performance and success of a team.

Participants

Up to 10 for each group

Procedure

1. Ask no more than 10 participants to form a circle. Give each participant a different color balloon and ask all participants to blow up their own balloons. Do not give any instruction on how large to blow it up. The colored balloon represents a type of job: professors, professionals, homemakers, or others.

2. Assign each person a separate number, 1 to 10, or however many are in the group.

3. Start the activity by asking participants to float their balloons in the air in front of them, keeping them afloat.

4. One by one, begin calling people by their number out of the circle, while their balloon "job" stays in the circle and must be kept in the air. For example: Ask number 3 and 5 to leave the circle.

5. Participants left in the circle must keep all balloons in the air, including the balloons from participants leaving the circle. Give the group a couple of minutes to reassemble to keep all balloons afloat.

7. Continue the exercise until half the people are left in the group and call "STOP."

9. Ask the group for observations and jot them down on a flipchart or whiteboard.
   What happened?
   What did the group try to do to keep all balloons in the air?
   How did you feel being responsible for so many moving parts?

Contributed by Erica Nelson, Nelson Performance Development, LLC

10. Give the participants remaining in the circle five minutes to debrief and develop a plan for what to do when another number is called out of the circle.

11. Restart the activity following the same pattern. After a period of time, call "STOP."

Debrief

- What adjustments did the circle make? Did the changes work?
- Were they able to keep the balloons in the air? Why or why not?
- Why was teamwork so important?
- What processes and practices do you use to build effective teams?
- How does the performance of one person impact the whole team?
- How important is effective communication? Why?
- What practices will you implement to build a stronger team?
- Identify next steps for implementation.

Variations

1. Have four to five extra balloons blown up and drop them in one at a time while the group is trying to keep their original balloons in the air.

2. The learning opportunity is to discuss how it felt to have the extra balloons drop in and relate it to their jobs with unexpected pressures, deadlines, new responsibilities, and so on.

Case Example

Used with a volunteer group to demonstrate that everyone has a role, but the most important role is ensuring that the team goals are met, even if it means picking up for others who may not be available to fulfill their role.

53   Decorate Your Cake and Eat It, Too

_____ Overview _____

Using teamwork and problem solving in a time-limited window, participants construct a four- to six-layer coconut cake.

Participants

Teams of two to eight can be grouped by position, department, or at random.

Procedure

1. Introduce the goal: to work together as a team to prepare a holiday coconut cake. Tell them that they have 20 minutes to complete the task.

2. Each team will select a supervisor. Say that only the supervisors from each team will be able to view the instruction sheet. The instruction sheet will be kept in the front of the room away from the teams.

3. Assign who will be on each team and provide the teams with their supplies, including: two cakes, coconut, Cool Whip, two cans of cream of coconut, large plate, sharp knife and dinner knife, dental floss, red and green dye, bowl for frosting, bowls for dyeing, spatulas, large spoons, can opener, paper towels, plastic wrap.

4. Tell them to work together following the instructions. The first team finished is the winner! But we all get to enjoy delicious cake at the end. Set the time for 20 minutes.

Debrief

- How comfortable were you with this task?
- Did your team work in sync?

_____

Contributed by Teri Rounsaville and Terry Lynn Hamm, Mississippi Association of Educators

- Did you build a new relationship?
- How important are following instructions?
- What would you do differently next time?

Variations

1. A variety of decorations can be made available.
2. Could be completed with five-minute relays of members stepping in and out of the process.
3. Aprons are helpful!

Case Example

This activity was used during a three-day staff meeting to go outside the dull meeting environment and to introduce teamwork. Many men were involved who weren't very comfortable in the kitchen. It took place in December and was called a Holiday Baking Team Building Activity.

These are the instructions:

1. The team should split up the tasks: cutting cake into layers, coloring coconut with food coloring, mixing frosting, soaking cake with cream of coconut, constructing the cake, frosting the cake.
2. Place a small amount of coconut in small bowls and dye red and/or green by using just a small amount of food coloring for decorating if desired.
3. Prepare frosting by stirring together cool whip, one cup of coconut, one-quarter can of cream of coconut.
4. Use two cakes. To create four layers, use either a knife or dental floss to cut the cakes into two even layers.
5. Level top of cake if needed.
6. Start building. With first layer in place on plate, poke holes with end of sharp knife, spoon about one-quarter can of cream of coconut over each layer.

7. Spread frosting on top of cake layer only.

8. Place next layer and repeat holes, pouring cream of coconut and frosting.

9. Continue until all layers are in place and complete.

10. Frost sides of cake.

54   Construct Your Team

Overview

Use this activity to reinforce the importance of accepting diversity within teams, the "it takes a village" concept. It would also work as a project management exercise.

Participants

Best for 15 or more participants with about 5 people per group

Procedure

Materials needed

- Observations note sheet for designated group observer
- Copy of rules for each table
- Flipchart paper and markers for each group

1. Prior to the session, purchase the same Lego™ kit for each team plus one for the facilitator. Remove the Legos from the original box and place them into a Ziploc bag. You do not want participants to see the finished design in color. Note: Be sure to make note of the number and type of pieces on each container; this makes disassembly easier. Complete one design for the facilitator and place inside a box or behind a barricade so participants cannot view it. Print black-and-white copies of the finished product for each team.

2. Assign teams which include no less than five and no more than eight people (Note: Groups with less than five people do not promote the appropriate debate and collaboration required for this activity).

3. Ask participants to determine who is going to be the observer and notetaker.

4. Pass out the kits, telling the group not to open them yet.

Contributed by Shannon Tipton, Learning Rebels

5. Explain the rules, being purposefully vague:

   ◆ Designated observer and notetaker may not speak or offer assistance; they are to observe group dynamic and process.

   ◆ Exercise is broken into three parts: planning, execution, and debrief.

   ◆ Only one person at a time from each group may examine the completed design; they may NOT pick up the piece or write down notes.

6. After explaining the rules give each group one black-and-white copy of the finished design. The group may ask and receive more copies, but do not offer this piece of information. (During the debriefing, this is a great opportunity to drive home "asking for guidance.") Tell them the total time for the exercise including planning is 30 minutes.

7. At the signal the group enters into the planning stage.

   a. Group may NOT take pieces out of container.
   b. Group may NOT see the completed design.
   c. Observer will make note as to how long the team takes to plan their course of action.

8. Once it is determined planning is complete, the team enters into execution.

   a. Once the group decides it has completed construction, you must sign off on the completed design with either a "yes" or "no."
   b. If yes: Groups are to stay intact until 30 minutes are up; do not get up and wander around.
   c. If no: Group must keep trying. Facilitator note: Do NOT give further direction. Group as a team will need to figure out what was incorrect about their design.

9. Once time is up, move into the debriefing and ask the observers to provide feedback to the group regarding their interactions as a team.

Debrief

• How did the length of time in the planning stages affect the overall execution of the design development?

• What was the dynamic of the group during the execution stage? Collaborative or autocratic? Explain.

- How could the collaborative process have been improved within the group?
- Did a leader emerge? Why did this person emerge as the leader? What were the identifiable traits?
- How did this exercise relate to the day-to-day teamwork within your department?
- What will you:
  - ◆ Keep doing
  - ◆ Stop doing
  - ◆ Start doing

Variations

1. To save time use a less complex design and allow a shorter time frame. The key is to keep pressure on.

2. If you have the time, group the participants in like categories, for example, senior managers or directors, to display a different dynamic that will demonstrate the need for different points of view within teams.

3. Exercise focus can be adjusted to target specific group need: shared vision, building trust, collaboration, communication/debate, focus on results.

4. If you use this exercise repeatedly, you may want to glue the pieces together for future use.

Case Examples

1. In a session targeting communication skills (rather than teamwork) the following questions could be asked during debriefing:
  - ◆ How did the group exhibit open communication techniques?
  - ◆ Give examples of how the group exhibited active listening techniques.
  - ◆ How did the group interact with each other? Was everyone given a voice?

2. In a session targeting new supervisors this exercise could demonstrate the value of understanding diverse opinions.
  - ◆ How can this exercise help you in managing a new team?
  - ◆ Describe how you handled conflict or disagreement in the group.

55   What's Your Story?

Overview

> This learning technique connects virtually any training topic with the personal
> stories of participants. Its goal is to connect personal experiences to training top-
> ics. The stories and the reflection related to the stories make the learning memo-
> rable. This technique can have impact. It connects the art of storytelling and the
> power of reflection to real business strategies or training needs such as team build-
> ing, diversity, and conflict or customer service.

Participants

10 to 40 participants (intact team or similar jobs)

Procedure

1. Use a PowerPoint slide, a flipchart, or a handout to draw a square divided into
   quadrants. The top two quadrants have business questions related to the topic. The
   bottom two quadrants have personal questions related to the individual. Examples
   shown.

Topic	Upper Left Quadrant	Upper Right Quadrant
Team Building	What is the best team you were ever on, and why was it the best?	What is the worst team you were ever on, and why was it the worst?
Customer Service	Describe a stellar customer experience you've had. Why was it stellar?	Describe an unremarkable customer service experience you've had. Why was it not special?
Diversity	What is you earliest recollection of a time when you were made to feel different?	Describe a time in your adult life when you went out of your way to include someone who was being left out or marginalized.
Conflict	Describe a time when you were involved in a conflict at work and it didn't turn out well. Why do you think that happened?	Describe a time when you were involved in a conflict at work and it turned out well. Why do you think that happened?

Contributed by Amy S. Tolbert, PhD, CSP, ECCO International

Topic	Lower Left Quadrant	Lower Right Quadrant
Team Building	What are you most proud of in your life?	One of the most surprising moments in your life was…
Customer Service		
Diversity	If you had one "do-over" what would that be?	What is "X" to you? (Truth, fairness, fun, crazy, hysterical, etc.—pick one word to present)
Conflict	What is one of your most powerful childhood memories that helped shape who you are today?	Who was the first love of your life? (Kindergarten, current relationship, or chocolate?)
	If you could share a meal with someone (*anyone* living, dead, or fictitious) tonight, who would that be and why?	Who was a mentor who has influenced you—and what does that person mean to you?
	Where did you grow up?	Describe the three happiest days of your life.

2. Divide participants into small groups of four to five people. Keep time for the group to keep the process on track.

3. Give each person three to four uninterrupted minutes to share their personal story. They can cover all of the questions or just focus on one. Whatever is most comfortable. Demonstrate answering all four questions to give an effective model and example.

4. After each person shares his/her story, the rest of the small group is given one minute to respond using the following guidance:

   ◆ Share something about that story that stood out for you.

   ◆ How does that story provide additional insight into today's training topic?

   ◆ What do you value in what you just heard?

5. Everyone must share. Everyone must respond to each story that is shared.

6. Bring the group together and ask for a few participants to share the best/worst (upper two quadrant questions) stories with the large group. Incorporate key points into the training topic and refer to the examples throughout the session.

Debrief

After every participant takes a turn, debrief with:

- What did you like about that activity?

- What did you learn from it?

- What did you learn about your colleagues that you did not know?

- How do you think what you've learned in this activity will impact your teamwork?

- What did you learn that sets the stage for our topic today?

Variation

Create a more general version, such as a "getting to know you" activity, and include general company-related questions in the top two quadrants, and the personal questions on the lower quadrants. Upper quadrant questions could include:

- What is one thing that you've done at work to earn somebody's trust? Share a story.

- What was your favorite project and why?

- What was your least favorite project and why?

- What do you think would make your workplace more effective? Share a story.

- Give an example of a time when you put the team's needs above your own for the good of the project/organization as whole (over your personal agenda). What was the result? What did that take of you?

Case Example

With an intact group of 12 people, this technique was used to enable participants to get them to know each other at a deeper level. The team did not break into groups, and instead shared their stories with all 12 individuals. The sharing caused laughter and tears in a short amount of time, primarily due to the validating feedback statements.

As a facilitator, this technique helps to identify what is already known about a subject before the in-person instruction begins.

Tools to Facilitate Active Learning

Energizers

Energizers are brief activities, exercises, or brain teasers that "energize" or motivate when the group's energy is ebbing. They may be used as a relaxer after a tense discussion, to get the cobwebs out following an extended period of information absorption, or during the post-lunch blahs. Try some of the activities in this section for creative ways to introduce and revitalize your sessions. All can be used for a variety of topics and customized to meet your needs.

56   Guess to the Beat

Overview

This energizing activity will help team members or colleagues get to know each other.

Participants

Newly formed team or work group of 20 maximum participants

Procedure

1. Before the session, ask participants in advance (privately) for two things: the name of their favorite song and what interests them most about their work. Download the songs from iTunes, following copyright guidelines. Create a separate slide for each participant identifying what interests each person the most about work. Also, create a "cheat sheet" for yourself with each participants name, song name, and job interest.

2. Announce that this is a combination of Name That Tune and Name the Person. Play the song and ask, "Can you name this tune?" At the same time display the PowerPoint slide that lists what interests the person most on the job. The person's name should not appear on the slide. Ask participants if they can identify this person.

3. You will probably not want to present all of the songs at the same time. Sprinkle them throughout the session, perhaps saving the most unlikely or the most interesting until near the end.

Debrief

- What was most surprising about your colleagues?
- What new information did you learn about each other?

Contributed by Eileen McDargh, McDargh Communications

- How can you use each other's interests in completing your work?
- Who might be a future "go-to" person for you?

Variations

1. This activity does not need to be used only for team building. It is an effective way to build fun into a department off-site meeting.

2. Allow yourself to have fun with this, too. You could ask for other "favorites" as well, such as pet, vacation, book, fictional character, movie, or many others.

Case Example

This was used with a team of world class performers who couldn't play well together. Music became the theme for the entire off-site meeting. Most people only know each other by title and job description. When the only attorney in the group had a favorite song that was a "head song" from the 1960s, people saw another side of him that transpired into much kidding and laughter. Given the other questions they also found out what part of his work held the most interest. It was an enlightening, light-hearted, yet meaningful exchange that brought the team together quickly.

57   Take a Stand

Overview

Use this strategy in a classroom setting to get people on their feet while accomplishing a secondary purpose such as an icebreaker, energizer, getting learners to "take a stand" on an issue, or getting group feedback.

Participants

Best for 10 to 50 people in a room with enough space to stand and walk around (not theater style).

Procedure

1. Display a question and two to four multiple choice answers.

2. Tell participants that they can indicate their answer by going to the part of the room assigned to each choice. For multiple choice point out what part of the room is A, B, C, or D.

3. Tell participants to go to the letter that matches their answer choice.

Debrief

- How do you explain the percent of people in each group at each answer?

Variations

1. Give the small groups each gathered around one response a task that can be done while standing together. The task may be related to their answer choice. For example you could ask them to determine the top reasons why their answer is best.

2. Ask participants to stand in their spot, add a "what if" element to the question and ask if they would move/change their response.

Contributed by Lisa MD Owens, Training Design Strategies, LLC

3. You could post the numbers 1, 2, 3, 4, 5 and ask a question that has a Likert Scale answer. For example, 1 = strongly disagree and 5 = strongly agree. Request that participants stand by the number that represents their answer. Comment on the number of people in front of each number. If they formed a line, it would be a human graph.

Case Examples

1. Used as an icebreaker: At a leadership training class for 30+ adult leaders at a national training site, we asked how far people had traveled to get to the session and indicated that the right wall = less than 100 miles, left wall = 100 to 500 miles, and the back of the room = more than 500 miles. While in the small groups, the participants listed on a chart pad the cities people came from. Then we asked, "How would you describe your level of experience with this topic?" The possible answers were none, some, or quite a bit). While in the small groups, the participants discussed what they wanted to get out of the course and wrote it on a chart pad for the trainer to see.

2. Used for feedback/Level 1 evaluation: The numbers 5 through 1 are written on the whiteboard at the front of the room with words underneath: Excellent, Very Good, Good, Fair, Poor. Learners are asked, "As you think about your experience so far today, how would you rate the experiment." The majority of learners line up by the 4, with a few at other spots. When asked again at the end of the day, most learners were at the 4 and 5. Alternative question: "Given what you have experienced today, how much better do you think you can do this (task, skill, procedure) where 1 is same as before and 5 is very much better than before."

58   Why I Like

Overview

Participants choose their favorite season and determine why they like it as a group.

Participants

Works well with up to 40 participants

Procedure

1. Place four words indicating seasons on four sheets of paper: Winter, Spring, Summer, Autumn. Place each on a different wall or area where participants can gather forming a small group.

2. Ask participants to choose their favorite season and walk to the word.

3. Tell them to discuss why they like their chosen season. Together they are to decide on a way to spotlight that season. They can sing a song, chant, cheer, recite a poem (original or not), or anything else that they choose. Tell them that they have seven minutes to get ready to spotlight the season they like.

4. After seven minutes ask each group to perform their season's "show" to the group.

5. Applaud and cheer loudly for each group.

Debrief

- What did you find in common with a new acquaintance?
- What result did planning and performing the show have?

Contributed by Teri Rounsaville, Mississippi Association of Educators

Variations

1. Many choices and variations are possible: kinds of music (blues, classical, pop, country); vacation destinations (mountains, beaches, desert, cities); TV programming (sitcoms, sports, police stories, reality shows).

2. If a group is too large, it can be split into two groups to complete the activity.

Case Example

Each season name was written on newsprint and decorated with clip art to define the season, for example, falling leaves for autumn. Once participants discussed why they like the season they selected, the performance ideas seemed to fall into place.

Experiential Learning

The experiential learning process is often used by facilitators to ensure that learning occurs and that learners are ready to perform on the job. Participants learn inductively; that is, they discover for themselves by experiencing the activity. The five-step process includes experiencing or doing something; sharing observations, feelings, and thoughts; interpreting the concepts; connecting what was experienced to real life; and planning ways to apply what was learned. The last four steps occur through a debriefing process which is why almost every activity in this book includes debriefing questions. It is critical to ensure transfer of learning. Each of the activities in this section models the concepts of experiential learning and can easily be adapted to any topic.

59   Appreciative Inquiry for a Positive Approach

Overview

Use appreciative inquiry at the beginning of a session or module to lay the foundation for future discussions and action planning.

Participants

15 to 50 in most learning situations

Procedure

1. Have participants pair off. Provide a list of the questions you have prepared for the session. See the cases for examples. Have participants respond to the specific written questions that ask about a successful past experience and, based upon that experience, what the participants would like to do or see occur in an upcoming similar situation (their wishes).

2. Tell them to take turns sharing a specific positive experience that relates to the learning content. Say that each person has ten full minutes as the speaker while the other participant serves as the listener/interviewer. They will then change roles.

3. State that the specific expectations for the listener include:
   ◆ Focus solely on the speaker's experience and feelings, and the details of the story.
   ◆ Actively listen to the speaker and probe for additional information.
   ◆ Allow for silence if the speaker needs to gather his or her thoughts.
   ◆ Hold your reactions and feelings until both have told their stories.

4. When the 20 minutes of paired dialogue is over, have the pairs share and discuss their conclusions (typically their answer to the last question).

5. Ask them to write their answers on the question page.

Contributed by Deborah Spring Laurel, Laurel and Associates, Ltd.

6. Combine two or three pairs to form a group of four to six and ask them to create a statement that incorporates key wishes.

7. Have them post these statements on a flipchart for the larger group to discuss and ultimately select one statement or two statements.

Debrief

- How did you like this activity?

- What did you learn that will help you (manage stress, create a motivational climate, etc.)?

- What is one action that you can take immediately?

Variations

Instead of debriefing the pairs, have the individual participants write their conclusions on flipcharts around the room. Then either:

- Read what was written, to identify common themes or strategies; or

- Have the participants walk around the room to read what was written on the flipcharts and write down on a worksheet the ideas that are most relevant to them.

Case Examples

1. In a motivation session for managers, the participants could be asked to answer the following questions:
   - Tell about a time when you experienced positive energy that was infectious. What was the situation? What created the positive energy? How did it feel to be a part of it? What did you learn?
   - If positive energy were the flame of your organization:
     1. How would you spark it to get it started?
     2. How would you fuel it to keep it burning brightly?

2. In a change management training, you could ask the participants to answer the following questions:

♦ Tell about a time when you handled a stressful situation well. What was the situation? How did you handle it?

♦ What helped you to successfully manage this stressful situation?

♦ Based upon this experience, what can you do in the future when faced with a stressful situation?

60   Exploring a New Frontier

Overview

Use this strategy to initiate a discussion of how learners feel about the unknown and having to try new things at work or personally. It promotes group discussion and internal reflection, and reinforces differences in how people react to change or dealing with the unknown. Can be done either face-to-face or virtually.

Participants

One to 50 or more in most learning situations

Procedure

1. Direct learners to draw the following items (per your instructions) on a flipchart, PowerPoint slide, whiteboard, or in participant's materials.

   ◆ With eyes open, using your primary/dominant hand, draw a pineapple.

   ◆ With eyes open, using your nondominant hand, draw a fish.

   ◆ With eyes closed, using your primary/dominant hand, draw a mushroom.

   ◆ With eyes closed, using your nondominant hand, draw a flower.

2. Ask participants how they felt when they had to do something with eyes opened but not using their dominant hand. What did they feel when performing the tasks with their eyes closed?

Debrief

• What happened? How did you feel when performing the tasks with your dominant hand? What about with your nondominant hand? Eyes closed?

• How did this experience help you understand how you feel about doing things differently than you've been accustomed?

Contributed by Lynn Lewis, Learning Solutions, LLC

- How will you use what you learned about yourself and how to react to change, the unknown, or trying something new?

- How will you use what you learned about how others react to change, the unknown, or trying something new?

Variations

1. You can debrief as a large group or in smaller breakout groups.

2. Invite the group to brainstorm ideas for how to help others with the unknown on projects or when rolling out new learning solutions.

Case Example

In a session for managers, you could use these questions:

- What can you do to help employees embrace change and new tasks?

- What types of reactions might you expect from employees when this change is introduced and implemented?

- What can you do to provide more information up-front to reduce anxiety about the unknown?

- What can you do to make the experience more engaging to help learners embrace change/the unknown and realize the full value/potential of the project's goals?

I've seen this activity used in some of the ATD classes that Lou Russell has conducted. I have also used it personally prior to seeing it. If there is an original author, I'd like to give credit because it is a great activity.

61   Let's Learn by Drawing

Overview

> Use this strategy to illustrate the importance of alignment and organizational systems design. In drawing, all of the elements must fit together as integrated parts of the whole image. The same principle applies to systems design.

Participants

Five to fifty participants

Procedure

1. Solicit a volunteer from each table. That volunteer serves as the model.

2. Everyone at the table draws the model.

3. After the drawing is finished, everyone walks around and looks at each drawing and determines which ones are the best.

4. The group then analyzes why.

Debrief

- Why are some drawings better than others?

- Why do the elements align more effectively in the better drawings than in the others?

- How does the principle of alignment in drawing relate to the alignment in business?

Variation

Invite someone who has drawing skills or tap someone from the class. After the group reviews the drawings, have them gather around the "artist" and watch the artist complete a portrait. The artist explains the methodology that they see and the importance

Contributed by Stewart Liff, Stewart Liff & Associates, Inc.

of looking at each element of the drawing (the eyes, nose, mouth, etc.) in relationship to each other.

Case Example

I use this as my icebreaker when I introduce the concept of visual management or systems alignment. The idea is to push people to think holistically and to begin looking at things from a systems-wide perspective, rather than looking for someone to blame. People seem to enjoy this because for the first time, they see how business and the arts both intersect and can support each other.

62   Lunch Bunch

Overview

Use this strategy for participants to learn more about each other before a learning intervention or starting a project together.

Participants

A maximum of five groups with four to six participants each

Procedure

1. Brief participants on the tasks and how building synergy will help the group to perform effectively.

2. Assign participants to groups of four to six and explain the goals of the activity.

3. Inform the participants that they will have lunch together at a place of their choice. They will leave at 11:00 a.m. and return by 2:00 p.m: Tell them that this time is being provided so that they can get to know each other better.

4. Provide each participant with a note pad and pencil and the guidelines on what to observe during the process.
   During the process:
   ◆ Observe what is going around you, especially your interactions with your group members.

   ◆ Make assumptions about the group members about their attitudes, personalities, and interests.

   ◆ Observe the various processes: choosing the place to eat, the choice of food, the conversations, how the payment was completed, the leadership and group processes, and the roles assumed by individuals.

   ◆ Take notes as needed.

5. On returning, allow the small groups 15 minutes to discuss what they each observed. Have them create a "shared" statement about their experiences.

Contributed by Mohandas Nair, Consulting, India

6. Ask a member of each of the small groups to share their observations. Use the guidelines you provided to guide the discussion.

7. After all groups have reported out, use the debriefing questions to summarize.

Debrief

- How similar were the experiences of each small group to yours? Why?

- What reservations did you have about the activity? Why?

- What was it like to be a part of the small group for lunch? The large group now?

- What questions do you have for the group?

- What are your hopes for this group/team?

- What suggestions do you have for how we can build upon what happened in the group experience?

Variations

1. Have only one group with a maximum of 12 participants.

2. Have a shorter activity like playing a game together, watching a short movie and discussing its learning, or sharing each other's personal issues to solicit empathy.

Case Examples

1. In a session on leadership skills you could use these questions:
- Share something about the person who made a difference in your life.

- Discuss the role of a leader. What is most important?

- What is the difference between the role of a manager and a leader?

2. In a new project team you could ask:
- Why do we need to work together? How did the lunch event help that process?

- What skills did you uncover that will be useful to accomplishing this project? Who possesses these skills?

- What do you think this team will need to be cautious about?

- What will be easy for this team?

63   QR Code Scavenger Hunt

Overview

The activity uses QR codes to take individuals to various resources. This is beneficial for new hire orientations or organizations that are restructuring activities in which leadership roles have changed.

Participants

This activity is most fun when the participants are in groups of four to seven. Each group must have at least one member who has a smartphone to scan the QR codes.

Procedure

1. Before the session: Create a list of the locations or people that you want the participants to visit. If your list includes people, be sure to brief those individuals on what information that they will provide to the participants in the activity. (They may provide a mini-training activity, a summary of their role, instruction on how to use their department's services, or some other information.) Also, share a tutorial on how to scan the QR code so they can help if participants encounter difficulty during the scavenger hunt.

2. Create a QR code using the "text option" on a QR creation tool like http://qrcode .kaywa.com/. Remember to number them when you print them out on note cards. The first QR code will be scanned when the group is created (that is the first clue), which will take them to the first location. Upon arriving at the first location, they will find the second location clue and so on.

3. During the session, split participants into groups of four to seven. Participants who do not have a wireless device should be placed in groups with others who have the technology.

4. Briefly explain QR codes and what they are used for to the participants. Have each participant download a QR code reader application on their device. Tell them that each QR code scanned will give them a clue to their next destination.

Contributed by Dr. Kella Price, SPHR, CPLP, Price Consulting Group

5. Ask each participant to scan a test QR code to ensure their devices are working properly.

6. Give each group its first clue.

7. Give each group the appropriate amount of time to locate each item and return to the designated location. The time will vary depending on the number of QR codes, the information gathered at each destination, and the distance between locations.

8. Take 10 minutes to have some of the groups describe key learnings for their group during this activity.

Debrief

- What did you learn from this exercise?

- What resource is new to you that you didn't already know about?

- Are there any resources that were not introduced that you would include for other participants?

- What resource can you use when returning to the job?

Variations

1. This activity can support participants in locating and viewing resources on a particular topic. Decide what virtual resources you want the participants to access. Place resources at stations throughout a learning center. Decide what resources that you want the participants to view or experience. Make a list of these virtual resources; some of them may complement a physical resource like a book, map, or job aid. For example, if you are conducting a Train the Trainer and it mentions a book (like Elaine Biech's *Book of Road-Tested Activities*), you may have that book at the station for participants to look at. Next to the book, or even attached to the cover, could be a QR code that directs the participants to a YouTube commentary by Elaine, reviews of the book, or the ATD webpage to order the book. Create a QR code using the "text option" on a QR creation tool like http://qrcode.kaywa.com/. Use a variety of resources (videos, blogs, articles, images).

2. You may want to send participants a tutorial on how to download a QR code reader and scan QR codes.

Case Example

One station might include what is shown in Figure 13.1:

http://bit.ly/QRcodesEZ

Scan me to order your own copy!

Figure 13.1

64 Tie Your Shoe

Overview

Use this activity to demonstrate the importance of two-way communication in a learning (on-the-job) environment.

Participants

Any number at any level in any job

Procedure

1. Ask for two volunteers, one who has shoes with laces who will represent the "learner;" the other volunteer will be the "trainer."

2. Ask the learner to sit in a chair facing the other participants. Ask the learner to untie one shoe.

3. Tell the trainer to provide instructions to the learner about how to tie a shoe.

   ◆ The trainer may not use any hand motions.

   ◆ The learner follows the instructions exactly without modification and without assuming any next steps; the learner may not ask clarifying questions.

4. Allow five minutes for the pair to complete the task.

5. Debrief the exercise using the questions. Lead an applause for the trainer and learner.

6. Observe that no matter how simple a task may seem to the trainer, the learner will need complete guidance.

Debrief

• What did this exercise demonstrate?

• What would have helped the learner?

Contributed by Shannon Tipton, Learning Rebels

- What would have helped the trainer?
- How would a demonstration have been helpful?
- How does this relate to what happens on the job?
- What will you remember to do differently as a result of this demonstration?

Variations

1. After three minutes have a member of the audience "tag" the trainer and try to complete the task. Allow for others to experience the difficulty of only verbal instruction of a simple task too.

2. Having two chairs back to back creates another level of difficulty by taking away the ability to see the learner.

Case Example

1. New managers learning coaching techniques

2. Train the trainer application
   - Demonstrate the importance of learning delivery methods.
   - Demonstrate tell, show, do.
   - Understand that lecture rarely, if ever, is a successful learning method.

3. Effective Communication course
   - One way versus two way.
   - Demonstrates the importance of using all tools—verbal, body language and tone of voice.

Feedback

Whether your learners are just starting their careers or have a great deal of experience, they will require advice and ideas for personal development. Many of us are not as good at delivering feedback as we could be, even though we appreciate the value. If you have created a safe environment, feedback is easier for the giver and the recipient. The tools in this section make it easier as well.

65   Presentation Peer Review

---------- **Overview** ----------

Use this strategy to review presentations or other demonstrations in a learning session. It promotes team learning about giving presentations and how to give effective feedback.

Participants

4 to 40 in most learning situations

Procedure

1. Before the session, create an evaluation form for presentations or any kind of demonstration participants are expected to learn.

2. Hand out the evaluation form to each participant in the learning session, one form per presentation. Tell participants to use this form to evaluate each presentation they watch.

3. Allow the first individual or group to deliver their presentation.

4. Use a whiteboard or set up a flipchart on either side of the room. At the top of one whiteboard or flipchart, write "Strengths" and at the top of the other, write "Improvement Opportunities."

5. Begin by asking the presenter how the presentation went. How does the participant feel about what happened?

6. Open the discussion to the group to provide their evaluation of the presentation. Ask for strengths of the presentation first, followed by improvements. Write the comments from participants under the respective whiteboard or flipchart. Summarize the discussion and end with comments on strengths.

7. Allow discussion to ensue, particularly if there is conflicting feedback.

Contributed by Meghann L. Drury-Grogan, PhD, Fordham University

8. Provide your own evaluation after the participants to avoid biasing their responses.

9. Have the participants take a picture using their camera phone of the strengths and improvement opportunities, so they have a reference of what they can do better next time.

10. Repeat steps three to nine for each presentation.

Debrief

- How did you feel about writing feedback for your peers and delivering it publicly?
- How did this experience help you understand the importance of delivering feedback effectively?
- What did this experience teach you about presentation/demonstration skills?
- What observations did you make during our discussion of the feedback as a class?
- Did some feedback conflict, and if so, how did we resolve it?
- How will you use what you learned for your next presentation?
- How will you use what you learned about giving feedback?

Variations

1. Assign participants to smaller groups rather than everyone evaluating every presentation. Find breakout rooms for each group.

2. Assign someone to track the time for each presentation so you say on time.

3. Assign specific presentation criteria to individuals. One person could evaluate one of these: gestures, eye contact, use of filler words, use of visuals, rate/pitch/tone of voice. By doing this you will have general evaluations and specific evaluations of the delivery.

4. Allow the participants to redo their presentations in the next class after they incorporate the feedback they have received in this class.

5. Ask presenters if they would like to have someone video the presentation on the presenter's phone.

Case Example

In a session to review group presentations, each group was assigned a different group to evaluate. This allowed some of the observers to listen and learn without having to be prepared with an evaluation after every presentation. The same feedback was provided with the addition of how well they transitioned and how they worked together in a team presentation.

66 Skills Feedback Rubric

Overview

Use a skills feedback rubric to provide specific feedback to help participants learn or improve a skill.

Participants

Any number of participants and observers; it is best to have an observer for each participant.

Procedure

1. Provide information about and demonstrate the specific skills to be learned and practiced.

2. Design a skills feedback rubric that includes:

   ◆ Overall learning objective

   ◆ New skills with specific examples

   ◆ Accompanying skills with examples

   ◆ Ineffective skills with examples

   ◆ Comments

   ◆ Ways to improve

3. Design the rubric in a table format that includes space for the observer to write comments.

4. Print enough copies of the skills feedback rubric for all observers.

5. Have the observer watch the participant practice the skill and make notes on the skills feedback rubric. Following the demonstration ask the observer to provide feedback to the participant using the skills feedback rubric after the practice.

Contributed by Gary Wagenheim, Wagenheim Advisory Group, Canada

Debrief

- What did you notice about this experience?
- How did you feel about this experience?
- What did you learn about feedback?
- How will you apply what you learned from this experience?

Variations

1. Have participants and observers codesign the skills feedback rubric before the practice.

2. Change the rubric to reflect the specific skills being learned.

3. If all participants are learning the skill, switch roles between observers and participants after a practice session so everyone gets to practice and observe.

4. Instead of printing rubrics, write it on a whiteboard or flipchart, or use a PowerPoint slide.

Case Example

This is an example of a communication skills feedback rubric.

Participant _____ Observer _____ Date _____

Learning Objective: Improve two-way oral communication

New Skills	X	
Ask open-ended questions (what, how, why)	X	Many questions were close-ended and invited yes or no replies. For example…
Probing (seek additional information)	X	You asked for an example when she said…
Summarizing (provide a synopsis of the session)		

New Skills	X	
Provide new information	X	You added a new insight about the project
Accompanying skills		
Good eye contact	X	You may want to make more eye contact
Head nodding		
Ineffective skills		
Excessive talking without listening		
Comments	X	You asked too many closed-ended questions
Ways to improve	X	Practice using open-ended questions

Manage a Classroom

Ensure that your classroom maximizes active learning. "Managing" your classroom starts long before you walk in. Be prepared early enough so that you can greet participants at the door, welcome them, learn their names, and allow time for them to tell you something that is important to them. Create a successful experience for your learners by creating a safe haven and comfortable environment for learning. Finally, be prepared for difficult situations that may occur. Be sensitive to the "mood" of the room that is created by both the physical aspects as well as each participant's demeanor. The activities in this section address challenges of every sort including moving participants into groups, bringing participants back on time, addressing difficult participants and situations, and facilitating an environment that considers learners' needs outside the classroom.

67 | Case Sorter

Overview

Use this activity to help participants self-sort into teams, based on interest, for a case study activity that offers multiple options. It allows participants to have greater intrinsic motivation for the case study they work on but helps you keep down the actual number of case studies discussed so you can stay within tight timelines.

Participants

Any type or number of participants

Procedure

1. Develop multiple case studies or short scenarios illustrating various situations that relate to the learning objective for the module. For example, if learners are learning how to deal with various difficult conversations, provide a variety of difficult conversation scenarios to choose from: 10 to 20. Give each one a descriptive short title, such as "Coaching team member on repeated missed deadlines," that gives a sense of what the scenario is about. Assign each scenario a unique number or letter of the alphabet.

2. Prepare a flip chart page with the numbers or letters of the scenarios listed and a blank line to the right of each one. For example, #1 _____; #2 _____; #3 _____; and so on.

3. Tell participants to quickly scan all the titles (and only the titles) of the scenarios (give the page numbers where they can be found in the workbook) and ask them to select their top two or three that most interest them. Tell participants to jot down on a sticky note or piece of paper the corresponding scenario numbers/letters that go with each of their top choices. Allow about one to two minutes for this.

Contributed by Halelly Azulay, TalentGrow LLC

4. Tell participants that as soon as they've selected their preferred scenario, they can go to the posted flipchart and write their name next to their corresponding numbers/letters. Encourage all participants to complete this quickly. Take about two to three minutes to complete. All participants should have their name next to two to three of the listed scenario numbers/letters.

5. Depending on the amount of time available for debriefing scenarios and the total number of participants, pre-determine how many total scenarios you would like to select for this activity (two to six participants per scenario).

6. Once all participants have self-selected scenarios, you should be able to see groupings around the most requested scenarios. This should allow you to divide participants into small groups to work on a scenario they are interested in.

7. Assign participants to scenarios and give instructions for the rest of the activity: Take ____ minutes to read the scenario and answer the provided discussion questions, and then report out for ____ minutes per team, and complete with a whole room debrief as needed for ____ minutes.

Debrief

Provide relevant discussion questions for each scenario (or use the same questions regardless of the scenario).

Variations

You could assign colors to each scenario and give corresponding dot stickers to participants. They could use the stickers to select the scenarios. You would list their names, and they would choose the color dots. This will allow you to quickly see how many greens, reds, yellows, and so on, and select groups this way. This works best if you only have a small group of participants.

Case Example

In a session about navigating difficult conversations, you could have various workplace or contextually-appropriate scenarios where participants must apply workshop lessons to navigate the conversation for maximum effective transfer of meaning. Discussion questions may include:

1. What went wrong with this scenario?

2. If you could replay this scenario to be more effective, what would you have the actors say/do differently?

3. Assuming you cannot replay it, what would you suggest the actors say/do next?

68   Hijacked Presentations

Overview

This activity allows discussion and practice for what to do when someone takes over a presentation.

Participants

Appropriate for any number or level of employee who makes presentations to others, especially to those in higher positions of authority.

Procedure

1. Begin with what comes to mind when the participants hear the concept of a "hijacked presentation." Take a few comments and then mention that this is particularly problematic when their boss is present. After hearing participants' definitions, provide the following explanation so everyone has the same understanding concerning this concept:

    A hijacked presentation is when you are in the process of delivering a presentation to a group of any size and a member of the audience begins trying to take over the presentation, likely your boss or someone in a higher position of authority.

2. Ask participants how they handled these situations when this has happened to them in the past. Allow participants to share their experiences and feelings when their presentations were hijacked in such a way.

3. As a follow-up to the last question, ask participants how much more difficult these situations are when the "hijacker" is their boss or someone else in a position of authority. Share any experiences you may have had when your boss hijacked your presentation.

4. Explain that if a presentation hijacker is suspected, there are a number of different things that participants might do to mitigate this situation. Engaging in some

Contributed by Peter R. Garber, author

preventative actions before the hijacking takes place may be the best strategy rather than just waiting for these situations to occur if at all possible.

5. Have participants pair up where they are sitting. Have half the room discuss how to prevent it from happening and the other half discuss what seems to work.

6. Bring the group together and ask for ideas from the "prevention" pairs. List the ideas on a flipchart. Add these suggestions:

♦ If based on past experience you suspect someone who might hijack your presentation, you could talk to that person in advance and try to get an agreement on when and how he/she will interject during your presentation. You could share the presentation with the hijacker in advance and ask the person to allow you to present a number of slides and then give the floor to the person, formally giving him or her control over that part of the presentation.

♦ If the hijacker is your boss you need to be careful not to imply things about his/her expertise on the subject but rather ask that you be given the chance to make the main points of the presentation before he/she interjects.

7. Ask for ideas from the pairs who discussed what can be done after it occurs. Post these on a flipchart page and add these suggested comments to hijackers who appear with little or no notice:

♦ "If I could just finish these next few points, we will open the floor to questions and comments."

♦ "That's a very good point. Thank you. I am going to cover that in a few minutes in more detail."

♦ "Exactly. That point is coming up and I'd appreciate it if you could hold until I get there."

♦ "In the interest of time, let me make a couple more points to keep us on schedule."

8. Finally, point out that how participants physically position themselves when making a presentation may help prevent their presentations from becoming hijacked. The point is that the more formal that participants make their presentation, the less likely someone may feel comfortable interrupting it. Suggest that in potential hijacker situations it may be better to actually stand next to the screen where the presentation is being projected and control the slides remotely. You have the focus of the presentation on both you and the materials being projected.

Debrief

- How will you prevent these uncomfortable situations in the future?
- What reminders can you give yourself before your next presentation?
- What will you do differently the next time your presentation is about to be hijacked?

Variation

Ask a participant to share a presentation he/she may have on their laptop, which would be appropriate to present to the group. Assign someone (or more than one person) in the audience to begin hijacking the presentation. Have the presenter try to minimize or stop the presentation from being hijacked.

Case Example

I was giving a presentation to a group and my boss began hijacking my presentation from his seat at the conference table, which was made worse by the fact that I had made a point to stand up in front of the group rather than to remain seated at the conference table as most other presenters that morning were doing. My boss's actions particularly surprised me as he usually did not do this to me, but I realized that he was trying to make the point to the group that he was fully committed to the topic of the presentation. I found myself trying to strike a balance between allowing the boss to be able to provide his input (and support) and maintaining at least some control over my presentation (not to mention my dignity). I needed some of the ideas in this activity to address my boss.

69   Our Anthem

Overview

Use this strategy to bring learners back from a break or from small group activities. The anthem is a song that serves as their auditory cue that it's time to come back to the classroom/large group.

Participants

Unlimited

Procedure

1. Before the learning session starts, choose three or four songs that relate to the topic directly, indirectly, or in funny ways. Have those songs available via iTunes, YouTube, or other formats. Be sure you are following copyright laws to use these songs.

2. List the three or four songs on a whiteboard, flipchart, or PowerPoint slide.

3. Explain that the group will select an anthem or theme song and it will be played any time they are to return to the large group.

4. Have the audience vote for the song they think best reflects the group.

5. Play the song to bring the group back from an individual or small group activity or from a break.

Debrief

At the end of class, ask the group: based on your experience today, did we pick the right anthem? Why or why not?

Contributed by Wendy Gates Corbett, MS, CPLP, Refresher Training, LLC

Variations

1. You select the song instead of giving the group a choice.

2. Use all three or four songs instead of just one.

3. Use as a pre-session activity and have people vote before the class via an online survey. Use the winning song to start the session.

Case Example

1. In a session on team building, list the three songs below on a flipchart, whiteboard, or PowerPoint slide.
   - ◆ "We Are Family" by Sister Sledge
   - ◆ "A Little Help from my Friends" by The Beatles
   - ◆ "I'll Be There for You" by The Rembrandts

2. Have learners select their anthem.

3. Play the winning anthem whenever you need to call the group back together.

70   Managing Deep Resistance

Overview

This is a strategy that trainers can keep in their back pocket for those rare times when they face group resistance.

Participants

Any number in small groups of five or six people each

Procedure

Introduction: Every once in a while, even the most accomplished facilitators/trainers will face deep-seated, escalating resistance from a group. The growing resistance may be due to something the facilitator has inadvertently done, or it may be due to something negative having occurred to the group prior to the onset of the program. The program may start with the usual amount of resistance that you might expect at the beginning of any training or team-building program. The problem is that the resistance begins to escalate, regardless of the content, and begins to focus on you. The resistance is almost always aggressive or passive aggressive in nature, rather than being withdrawn. It might even reach the point of curtness or mild verbal abuse directed at the program or at you personally.

The best strategy is to address the situation as soon as you are aware of it. This might bring the causal factors to the forefront, and you can address them, work through them, and continue on with the scheduled program. Frequently, however, direct confrontation serves only to produce silence or denial on the part of the group which, in turn, results in the resistance increasing. When things reach this stage, usually the outcome is to abort the program or attempt to slog through as things

Contributed by H. B. Karp, Hampton University. Originally published as: H. B. Karp, "The Skilled Facilitator: Working with Deep Resistance," in *The 2003 Annual: Volume 2 Consulting*, ed. Elaine Biech (San Francisco: Jossey Bass/Pfeiffer), 67–70.

worsen. Either way, it ends up in a very painful experience for everyone involved. There is, however, an alternative.

1. Halt the program and explain to the group that you are aware that something seems to be severely amiss. Give some examples of what you are experiencing, for example, "No one is asking or responding to questions," "People have been getting up, walking out, and coming back randomly," or "The few things that have been said strike me as being curt, or even somewhat hostile in tone."

2. Ask the group if something is wrong, or if you have done something that might have produced this effect. If the answer is "Yes," find out what happened, respond to it, and then continue with the program.

3. If there is no clear answer to your question, ask each participant to write down a number that *right now* expresses his or her satisfaction with you and with the program up to this point, "1" being "Least Satisfied" and "10" being "Most Satisfied." Assure them that they will not be asked to disclose their responses.

4. Ask the total group to break out into small groups of five or six and select one member to be spokesperson for their group.

5. Once groups have formed, ask each group to brainstorm a list of items. Ask them to "Write down everything that you *do not like* about the program, about what we have been doing, or about me personally. Please be as specific as you can." Give the groups about five minutes to complete this task.

6. Ask the spokesperson of the first subgroup to read their list to you out loud. If met with hesitation, warmly assure the group that this is exactly what you want. Maintain good eye contact with the speaker, listen actively, and write down everything said on your notepad. When the list is completed, quickly read back the items presented, to make sure you have them all, and then thank the speaker. The only thing you may say is to ask for clarity on an item if you are unsure. Continue this process until all groups have responded.

7. When the feedback is completed, repeat the process; however, now ask the groups to brainstorm a list of everything that they *do like* about the program, the process, and you personally. Give them about three minutes to complete this task.

8. Repeat the feedback process in exactly the same manner as in the first report out.

9. When this is completed, ask everyone in the room to write down a number that *right now* expresses his or her satisfaction with you and the program up to this point, "1" being "Least Satisfied" and "10" being "Most Satisfied." Again, assure them that they will not be asked to disclose their responses.

10. If you choose to, you can ask the total group, "How many experienced a reduction in satisfaction?" "How many experienced no change?" "How many experienced an increase in satisfaction?" (The expectation is for no decrease and about a 20 percent increase in satisfaction.)

11. Respond to any "dislike" item from the first list that requires a response or an action.

12. Ask the group if they would like to continue with the program. If the answer is affirmative, take a 15-minute break and pick up the program when you get back.

13. Remember that the objective of this strategy is not to eliminate *all* the resistance. The objective is to eliminate enough of the unnecessary resistance to allow you to proceed slowly with the program.

Variation

This process can also be productively used as a training device in dealing with the topics of "resistance" or "change leadership." For it to be effective, the group must have a reasonable amount of experience working with you, for example, at the midpoint or later of a two- or three-day training program, or in the middle of a 6- to 15-week training or academic course.

1. Since the objective is to instruct, the exercise is sprung on the group with no warning. Ask them to write down a number expressing their individual satisfaction with you and the program up to this point, on the same 1–10 scale.

2. Ask the group to break out into small groups of five or six and select one member to be spokesperson for their group and to brainstorm a list of items that they *do not like* about the program, about what they have been doing, or about you personally. Ask the spokesperson of the first subgroup to read their list to you out loud. Maintain good eye contact with the speaker, listen actively, and write down everything said on your notepad. When the list is completed, quickly read back the items presented to make sure you have them all, and then thank the speaker. The only thing

you may say is to ask for clarity on an item if you are unsure. Continue this process until all groups have responded.

3. When you have thanked the spokesperson, after the "dislike" feedback, ask for the group's mean satisfaction score and post it on the board.

4. Repeat this process for the "like" feedback. After you have thanked the spokesperson for the "like" feedback, ask everyone to again rate the program on a 1–10 scale. Ask each spokesperson for the mean score and again post it on the flipchart.

5. When the process is complete you will have pre-post exercise data. You can discuss this now, or, preferably, wait until after you have presented the "resistance" part of the session.

71 Assigning Groups

Overview

Experience multiple ways to form groups; great for a train the trainer session or just an energizer.

Participants

Any number in a facilitation or train the trainer session

Procedure

1. This activity was created as an energizer for a train the trainer class. The purpose was to demonstrate very quickly multiple ways to form groups. So there is a valuable takeaway for trainers, facilitators, instructors, designers, and others in the profession. However, it can just as easily be used as an energizer for any class and a team builder if people need to learn some interesting facts about their team members.

2. Ask all participants to stand. Ask how many get bored with counting off to form groups or working with their same table groups. After most raise their hands, say that they are about to experience an idea dump of several ways to form groups in their next sessions.

3. Say that you will identify "groups" and they are immediately to walk to the defined group. Tell them that they will not have much time because every 30 seconds you are going to state new groups and they should move quickly to the new group. Also, add that the divisions will be for two, three, four, and five teams.
   - For some reason, people (in the U.S.) have strong feelings about peanut butter. So, it is fun to ask people which brand they prefer. So for five teams, point to a spot for each of the peanut butters: Jif Chunky, Jif Smooth, Skippy Chunky, Skippy Smooth, or those who do not like peanut butter.

Contributed by Dawn Mahoney, CPLP, "Learning In the White Space," LLC

- ◆ For three teams: Coca Cola, Pepsi, or no soda at all.

- ◆ For four teams: who has been in the workforce less than 5 years, 5 to 10 years, 10 to 20 years, over 20 years?

- ◆ For four teams: who is wearing brown tie shoes, brown slip-on shoes, black or white shoes, other color shoes?

- ◆ For three teams: who ate a home-cooked dinner at home, who ate fast food, who ate out last night?

- ◆ For two teams: who played sports in high school and who did not play sports in high school?

- ◆ For four teams: oldest, youngest, middle, or only child in your family.

- ◆ For three teams: your preference is for chocolate candy, other candy, no candy.

- ◆ For two teams: thick or thin crust pizza.

- ◆ For three teams: who has written a book, who would like to write a book, who wants nothing to do with it?

- ◆ For two teams: who has received a speeding ticket and who has not?

- ◆ For five teams: if the last digit of your phone number is a 1 or 2, 3 or 4, 5 or 6, 7 or 8, 9 or 0.

- ◆ End with two teams: who is having fun and who is not having fun?

4. Now it's their turn. Ask participants for ideas. Have them shout out the ideas and move to where they point.

5. Once you've exhausted all the ideas from the group, lead a round of applause for everyone.

Debrief

- Which ideas were new to you?
- What questions do you have about forming groups?
- Which ways to form groups will you use?

Variations

1. Change the list to some of your own. Present at least 10 ways, which will take you less than 10 minutes.

2. After the groups or pairs have been determined and relocated, you may sometimes need to determine who goes first, who leads, or who the spokesperson is. There are multiple ways to do this. Instead of the commonly used recent birthdays, get creative and try using items like the following:

- Whoever has eaten tacos in the past week
- Names that begin with the letter (pick one)
- Prefers vanilla ice cream
- Hates to play BINGO
- Has learned to ride a horse
- Prefers their Hershey's candy bars with almonds
- Cooked dinner the previous evening
- Loves broccoli
- Can "Double Dutch" jump rope

72 How *Not* to Do It

<hr>
Overview

As part of a larger lesson on how to conduct a typical class, participants take part in a demonstration of how *not* to do it.
<hr>

Participants

5 to 10 new instructors

Procedure

1. After covering the basics of how to start, conduct, and end a learning session, divide the group into two teams. Tell them they have five minutes to work in their teams to come up with two or three ideas of how you do not want to start a class. (Remind them to keep it within acceptable norms of professionalism.)

2. After five minutes have them go to the front of the room, one team off to the left and one off to the right. In a "Who's Line Is It Anyway" (improvisation) format, call on them to alternate one person per team to come give a 5 to 15 second demonstration. Provide lighthearted feedback.

3. After everyone has had a chance, tell them to go back in their groups and in five minutes come up with how not to end a class.

4. After five minutes have them go to the front again, and ask for short demonstrations from each person.

5. Lead a thunderous applause for all the actors.

Debrief

- How many of those looked like classes you've actually been in?

- Have you ever done any of those for a class or a presentation you've led?

- What will you do to ensure you don't do anything like that?

<hr>

Contributed by Christopher Mortenson, CM Success Solutions

Variations

1. Ask individual participants to demonstrate one thing to avoid when opening a session in one large round without any planning. Do the same for closing a session. Repeats are okay.

2. Stand in two lines facing each other. One side says what they should do; the other line says what they should not do in the same case. After round one, reverse who states what a trainer should or should not do to start or end a learning session.

Case Example

This activity was run for several courses in the Academic Instructor Course at the Air Force's National Security Space Institute in Colorado Springs. I acted as the emcee of the lesson, really hamming up the "Who's Line…" persona. Once one of my students went to the front and did an all-too-convincing impersonation of me of how I had begun the previous day when I had had a frustrating morning. It gave everyone a good laugh, even me.

73 Critical Connections

Overview

> Participants may be distracted when issues back on the job arise that need to be addressed. This strategy introduces a process to relieve some of the anxiety so participants can be fully present to learn.

Participants

Unlimited; works with any group of people within the same organization

Procedure

1. State that people often find themselves attending training sessions alongside others with whom they have a work-related issue to discuss. Moreover, "hot" issues often arise that need to be addressed that day, leading to anxiety on the part of participants who can feel torn between being an active session participant and not letting anything "fall through the cracks" or go unaddressed because they are out for training. To take advantage of the serendipity of being in the same place at the same time and relieve the anxiety of when to address pressing issues so people can be fully present for training, we want to lead a brief review of Critical Connections.

2. Turn to a prepared flipchart page with "Critical Connections" at the top.

3. Ask the group, "Is there someone in the room with whom you need to connect briefly during a break in the session to discuss a work issue?"

4. As people announce their connections, write the name of the person who is asking for the connection, and a double arrow ($\leftarrow\rightarrow$) to the name of the person with whom they want to connect.

5. Encourage people to individually note those who want to connect with them and be responsible for managing those connections during the course of the day.

6. Announce when break times are available so that people can mentally plan their connections.

Contributed by Dennis DaRos and Tara Whittle, The Kaleel Jamison Consulting Group, Inc.

7. Participants should be self-responsible for crossing their connection off the list once it has been made.

Debrief

At the end of the day refer to the Critical Connections:

- Did you meet with your connection?
- Was this helpful?
- How might you use this in meetings in the workplace?

Variations

1. Take a five-minute break immediately after soliciting the Critical Connections to allow people to make quick connections or share information or pass tasks/requests to others that might lessen the urgency of the connection.

2. As so often happens when people take time away from their daily work for training, urgent issues can arise that require their attention. The Critical Connection process can incorporate "buddies." For instance, if one person needs to step out of an education session, she can ask another person to collect any materials on her behalf and brief her later on what she missed. The facilitator can create a "Buddy List" so that those who already know they will need to step away from the session can make their brief absence public and make everyone aware that they have contracted with someone to bring them up to speed. Participants can add themselves to the list throughout the session time if something unexpected arises.

Case Example

A recent session participant shared that she had an outstanding work issue that needed to be addressed and was glad to see the person with whom she needed to discuss the issue was in the same session. At the same time, she was anxious about how to find time to talk to this colleague, and worried about having her attention divided and not getting the most out of an important event she had cleared her calendar to attend. By using the Critical Connection process, she was able to make the request to talk offline and find time over an afternoon break to address the issue. Knowing a space had been made to have the conversation, she was able to be fully present throughout the day.

Stimulate Discussion

You know it is important to encourage dialogue and conversation to help participants sort through what is meaningful to them and what to implement upon the return to their workplace. Discussion allows participants to share expertise, get their questions answered, and hear another side of a topic. Good discussion can turn a negative attitude into a positive one. Ensure that you initiate discussion by building interest. Learn to ask clear questions and to be comfortable with silence as you await responses. You can't expect enthusiastic involvement if you always answer your own questions without waiting for responses. These unique strategies stimulate discussion.

74   What IF?

Overview

The What IF Game is designed to be a questioning tool to help presenters simulate discussion by refocusing this topic from a different perspective. It is intended to make participants think about the subject at hand in a different way than they may have ever thought of in the past.

Participants

This activity could be used with any number or type of employee who can contribute to the discussion.

Procedure

1. Introduce this activity as an exercise in trying to explore alternative options and more creative decision making.

2. Explain that it can be played as a sort of game with participants to stimulate their thinking and problem solving ability.

3. The What IF Game is actually easy to lead and play. It consists of you simply presenting a series of "What IF" scenarios to participants and challenging them to come up with solutions to problems that they may face at work. The more complex the What IF statement, the more challenging the solutions that participants may need to think of.

4. For example, it may be best to start with a relatively easy What IF scenario. Begin the game by asking participants what they would do in a simple situation such as running out of copy machine paper for their printer that they use at work. Participants would likely answer that they would simply go to their supply station to retrieve more copy paper. But now, begin presenting What IF scenarios such as, "What if there wasn't any more copy paper available at the supply source or station where you typically retrieve such a resource? Participants would now have

Contributed by Peter R. Garber, author

to think a bit harder to figure out where they would need to go or who to contact to get the paper they needed. The next What IF scenario could be "What if the next source of copy paper was also out of paper, what would you do then?" At this point, participants probably would immediately know what they would need to do. This is where the exercise begins to get creative and more fun. You could take this scenario to whatever extreme that you might want to, say for instance, "What if there was a national shortage of copy paper, what would you do to perform your job other than the way that you are currently used to performing the job." Participants would need to come with creative solutions to this national shortage by creating an enriched learning experience and thinking out of the box for sure.

5. Finding scenarios that directly relate to the participants' work world would be ideal and could create some creative and practical solutions to current problems in the workplace. Capture these ideas on a flipchart for possible future applications.

Debrief

After completing this exercise, ask participants which of their suggestions could be useful at the present time without the What IF scenarios presented and ask for ideas how these could be implemented.

Variation

Have participants create the What IF scenarios after explaining how this game is played.

Case Example

This was used with a hospital group to explore ideas and prepare for handling a natural disaster.

75   Brainstorm Debrief

Overview

Use this strategy to debrief any brainstorming activity. This works especially well with large groups and allows you to hear all ideas in a short period of time.

Participants

Unlimited—the more, the better

Procedure

1. Select any topic in which a group brainstorming discussion would be beneficial.

2. Divide into small groups (four to six recommended). Give each group markers and flipchart paper.

3. Ask the group to brainstorm the topic selected and to record answers on the flipchart sheet.

4. As each group finishes, have them post their flipchart sheet on the wall.

5. Ask each group to send one person to their flipchart to present for the group with a marker in hand.

6. Choose the longest list and have the group presenter read through their responses. Ask all other presenters to check off anything that the first presenter covers and tell them that they will not have to repeat what has already been stated. To keep everyone engaged, ask the presenter's group to help their presenter find duplicates as ideas are presented.

7. Continue presenter by presenter until all ideas have been stated (continue to check off duplicate ideas).

Contributed by Lorna J. Kibbey, Kibbey Leadership Solutions

Debrief

- Were you surprised at how many ideas were the same? Different?
- Which ideas were most often stated?
- What's next? What will we do with this information?

Variations

1. If time is limited, set time limits for brainstorming session or ask the group to list their top five.

2. Can be used as a precursor to a group selection technique such as nominal group technique (NGT).

Case Examples

1. In a retreat session for a large number of employees, ask for ideas to improve productivity. Use this activity to efficiently review all ideas.

2. In a session to teach leadership skills, ask groups to brainstorm and record common characteristics of great leaders. Use this activity to efficiently review all ideas and note the most common answers.

76   Quote Me

┌─────────────────────── **Overview** ───────────────────────┐

Use this strategy as an opener to get participants thinking about the topic. It can be used in a classroom setting to stimulate discussion or as an assignment between sessions in a multi-session course.

└──┘

Participants

4 to 20 in most learning situations

Procedure

1. Prior to the session, select a number of quotations that relate to the topic. Plan on one quotation for each group.

2. Print each quotation on a flipchart page and post the pages on the walls around the room.

3. Introduce the activity by explaining that you want to get participants thinking about the topic.

4. Divide the group into subgroups of four or five people.

5. Assign each subgroup a different quotation and ask the subgroups to get up and go to the posted quotation they have been assigned.

6. Give the subgroups 10 minutes to discuss the quotation as it relates to the topic and how they have seen the meaning of the quotation demonstrated in the workplace.

7. At the end of the designated time period, ask a representative from each subgroup to summarize their discussion for the rest of the group.

Debrief

- What was your reaction to the quotations?

- How relevant are the quotations to the topic?

Contributed by Karen Lawson, Lawson Consulting Group, Inc.

- Which quotation had the most meaning for you? Why?
- What was the benefit of this activity?
- How might you draw on these quotations in your role at work?

Variations

1. Instead of assigning one quotation per group, give each participant a quotation and ask each person to explain the assigned quotation in the small group.

2. In a virtual classroom, assign each person a different quotation and ask each person to post his or her responses in the discussion forum.

3. As an inter-session assignment, participants would present their interpretations of the quotations and personal examples to the rest of the group.

4. As a pre-work assignment, ask participants to choose a quotation relevant to the topic and come prepared to discuss the reason they chose that particular quotation.

Case Examples

1. In a session on leadership, you could do the following:

- ◆ Assign the following quotations:
  - ○ "You get the best effort from others not by lighting a fire beneath them, but by building a fire within."—Bob Nelson
  - ○ "The key to successful leadership today is influence, not authority."—Ken Blanchard
  - ○ "People tend to resist that which is forced upon them. People tend to support that which they help to create." —Vince Pfaff
  - ○ "Before you are a leader, success is all about growing yourself. When you become a leader, success is all about growing others."—Jack Welch
  - ○ "Outstanding leaders go out of their way to boost the self-esteem of their personnel. If people believe in themselves, it's amazing what they can accomplish." —Sam Walton

- Ask participants to respond to the following:
  - What does the quotation mean?
  - How does it relates to one's success as a leader?
  - Cite specific examples where they have observed this principle being applied (or not applied) in their workplace.

2. In a program on dealing with change, you could do the following:

- Assign the following quotations:
  - "We must become the change we want to see."—Mahatma Gandhi
  - "It is not the strongest of the species that survive, nor the most intelligent, but the one most responsive to change."—Charles Darwin
  - The difficulty lies not so much in developing new ideas as in escaping from old ones."—John Maynard Keynes
  - "Any change is scary, and when we are scared, we use our power of fantasy to come up with scenarios of disaster."—Dr. Arthur Freeman and Rose Dewolf

- Ask participants to respond to the following:
  - What does the quotation mean?
  - How does it relate to the topic of change?

77 Put the Idea on Trial

> ――――――――――――― **Overview** ―――――――――――――
>
> This involves using a mock jury trial to introduce or review information to a group. Utilize to make points pro and con in an interesting way. It can also be used as a recap or review or to present facts and gain understanding of issues.

Participants

Best with 20 or less to keep everyone involved

Procedure

1. Assign or ask for volunteers for roles in advance: judge, bailiff, defense attorney, prosecution attorneys, witness for the defense, and witness for the prosecution. The rest of the audience can be the jury.

2. For added fun, get props if desired: judge's robe or black table cloth, gavel or substitute.

3. Allow time for the attorneys to talk to their witnesses in advance.

4. Have the bailiff ask the audience to rise while the judge walks in.

5. Create a trial based on the example given.

6. Watch the timing. This will generally take a minimum of 30 minutes, but can get out of hand depending on how many witnesses and how many questions.

7. Wrap up the trial and lead an applause for the actors.

Debrief

- What salient points were made for the prosecution (name the charge)?
- What salient points were made for the defense (name the charge)?
- What was the turning point that contributed to your final decision?
- How can you use this information in the future?

―――――――――――――――

Contributed by Renie McClay, Inspired Learning, LLC

Variations

1. This is written for an American audience because it somewhat mirrors a U.S. trial, but could be revised for any judicial system.

2. This can be done in a classroom or in a synchronous online class.

Case Example

One place to use this is when looking at a competitive product. Here is an example script.

Bailiff: All rise. Court is now in session. Honorable Judge Susan presiding.

(The judge comes from outside the room looking serious or comical.)

Judge: Welcome to Business Court. This is the case of the questionable product. Bailiff, has the jury been impaneled?

Bailiff: Yes, your honor.

Judge: Who are they?

(Bailiff points to the jury: the whole audience or an identified couple of rows of people.)

Judge (opening comments): The jury is going to hear statements from the defense on the advantages of The Good Guys product line, which is being challenged by the competition. Council for the prosecution is seeking the death penalty for Product Line X. Your job is to hear the testimony and decide on the merits of Product X for yourself. If you are convinced beyond a shadow of a doubt that Product X is guilty as charged, you are to find it guilty and recommend a sentence. If not convinced beyond a shadow of a doubt that Product X is a worthless product, you should enter a verdict of not guilty. Ladies and gentlemen of the jury: Do you understand your charge?

Sequence of events:

- Prosecution's opening comments
- Defense's opening comments
- Prosecution calls first witness
- Defense cross-examines

- Defense calls first witness
- Prosecution cross-examines
- Prosecution's closing arguments
- Defense's closing arguments

Judge (closing comments): Ladies and gentlemen of the jury, the evidence has been presented on the legitimacy and value of Product X. Your job at this time is to render a verdict on the validity of this product. You are being asked to decide the guilt or innocence beyond a reasonable doubt. I am going to poll the jury at this time as to the guilt or innocence of this product. Jury, please raise your hand at this time if you agree with the prosecution and think that Product X should be put to death.

Those who feel not guilty?

The decision of the jury is final. (Pound the gavel.)

Closing and Follow-Up for Active Learning

Application

The purpose of training is to provide learners something that they can apply in the form of skills or knowledge back at the workplace. One of the critical requirements of a session closing should be to review the content and help participants determine how they will apply what they learned. Participants need time to reflect and review what they have learned, consider the challenges and the possibilities, and decide how they can apply it back on the job. Numerous ways to practice, analyze, and internalize the content are presented.

78   At Work in the Real World

Overview

This is a strategy that asks participants to apply the content to real situations in their workplace, while they learn it.

Participants

Best used with managers or individuals preparing to be managers in groups of 20 or less

Procedure

1. Hand out a 3″ × 5″ card to each participant.

2. Ask each person to write down a situation occurring (or that has occurred) in your workplace that represents a performance problem.

3. Collect the cards. Place everyone in small groups of two or three.

4. Redistribute the cards, making sure each group gets cards they didn't create.

5. Have each group discuss the situations and how they would handle them if they were the manager. They should write their recommendations on the card and prepare to present to the large group.

Debrief

- Was the situation your group received suitable for this topic?

- Ask the "author" of the scenario, "How would or how did your organization handle the actual situation?" Does that differ from the group recommendation? Why might that be?

- How do these kinds of problems affect the rest of the team? The organization?

- How could not addressing a situation like this affect the team or the organization?

Contributed by Barbara Crockett, independent contractor

Variation

Change the topic to a service problem, communication, or almost any other topic where you want participants to see how this applies to a real-life situation at work.

Case Example

I use this strategy when teaching a topic like progressive discipline. While participants learn about the steps (verbal warning, written warning, termination), this activity asks them to apply the steps to real situations in their workplace. Sometime there is a need to distinguish between a performance issue and a communication issue. One situation written was "an employee is wearing too much perfume." This really called for a conversation with the employee about the impact the scent was having on others on the team rather than discipline regarding performance of the employee. This strategy allows those discussions to occur.

79   Instant Editors

Overview

Use this strategy when participants are attending a learning session to gain knowledge for creating a written statement of some kind, such as a mission statement, a policy, or a competency model.

Participants

6 to 40 in a live classroom setting

Procedure

1. Ask participants to write an initial draft of their document.

2. Once they have a draft, ask the participants to find a partner to share it with and to receive feedback, including suggestions for additions or deletions of content.

3. After sharing with a partner, ask the participants to follow the same process with at least two other partners (for a total of three rounds), making edits to their drafts as they go.

4. When finished, ask the participants to write their final draft based on the input they received.

5. Ask for a handful of volunteers to share aloud with the whole group their newly-edited versions of their written item.

Debrief

- How different was your final (or most recent) draft from your first, based on the feedback you received?

- What are a few of the specific changes you made to your draft that you incorporated?

- What was helpful about this process?

Contributed by Lisa J. Downs, Development Wise Consulting

Variations

1. Have two pairs form small groups and pass the drafts from person to person to read and provide feedback.

2. Have a spokesperson from each small group share an example of a "finished" product.

3. Triads can also be used to allow for more input than a team, but less time than a quad.

Case Examples

1. In a manager training session, participants could write their expectations and/or norms for their teams.

2. In a leadership training session, participants could write a statement of what defines them as a leader (characteristics, values, how they interact).

3. In a session for entrepreneurs, participants could write what they stand for as their professional brand (what they do and why, their value proposition, who they serve).

80   Make It Stick

Overview

Use this strategy to capture how people will apply what they learn. Record actions to make them stick.

Participants

Any number of participants during a learning experience or team action planning discussion

Procedure

1. Post a flipchart or label a whiteboard, "How will you apply what you learn today?"

   ◆ Variation: "What actions will you take starting tomorrow?"

   ◆ Variation: "What new tasks do you have on your 'to-do' list?"

2. Invite participants to record actions on sticky notes throughout the learning experience or discussion. Make them stick on the flipchart or whiteboard.

3. Organize the sticky note actions by themes during breaks. Quickly debrief the actions after a break or lunch. This may sound like, "So far we have identified a dozen actions of how you will apply what we learned today to our daily performance such as_____. What additional actions might make a difference for you, your team, or your business?"

4. Invite participants to record additional actions and "stick" them to the chart.

5. Immediately after the experience, organize and type all of the actions. Distribute to the participants.

6. One month after the experience, redistribute the list of actions and ask participants to share "What difference did this make?" to the group. Provide an example if possible.

Contributed by Kimberly Seeger, MS, CPLP, Senior Talent Development Leader

Debrief

- What occurred when we captured your actionable ideas throughout the experience?
- How does this support your continuous learning beyond our time together?
- Who will help you remain accountable to complete the actions?
- What is the business impact if you complete all of the actions listed on this chart?
- Why is action planning a valuable strategy of learning?

Variations

1. Include who will do what by when on every sticky note to create project plans or accountability metrics.
2. As ideas are shared during a learning experience, encourage participants to convert to actions by restating or questioning the idea.

Case Examples

1. During a leadership development experience focused on coaching, you might identify specific actions such as:

   - Schedule a conversation with a direct report to discuss career opportunities.
   - Use the resources provided to plan a coaching conversation, monitor progress, and foster accountability.
   - Share what difference this makes to your people and business.

2. During a hands-on technology skill building experience, you might identify specific actions such as:

   - Update the Excel spreadsheet to include charts.
   - Talk to the team about using a shared Outlook calendar for scheduling organizational learning opportunities.
   - Develop a new SharePoint page for resource sharing.
   - Share what difference this makes to your people and business.

81 Application Action Plan

Overview

A strategy to develop action plans for application with help from other participants.

Participants

Any number for any session

Procedure

1. Ask participants to complete an action plan with these categories:

    ◆ Ideas or insights

    ◆ Areas to investigate

    ◆ Actions to take

2. Ask participants to make a list of steps to use their ideas or insights, or a list of steps to begin an investigation or steps to begin to take action.

3. Ask participants to make a list of barriers they anticipate when implementing each part of their plan.

4. Form participant groups of three to five and ask participants to share their plans and supporting lists. After participants present their action plans and lists of steps and barriers, others in the group offer additional steps and/or solutions to overcome barriers.

5. Facilitate a summary using some of the debriefing questions.

Debrief

• How did you feel as you developed your action plan?

• How did the group help you?

Contributed by Jean Barbazette, The Training Clinic

- What issues might arise when implementing your action plan?
- What are the consequences of ignoring what you have learned in this session?
- What is one 'ah-ha' that you are taking away from today's session that you can implement tomorrow?

Variation

This activity could be completed in pairs. The pairs establish a time for a follow-up call one to two weeks from today.

Case Example

Following a time management class, a participant was so excited about the value of the action plan and what he was able to accomplish by implementing his plan, he volunteered to teach the next time management class his company offered.

Closing Practice
and Review

Bringing closure to a training session is a lost art. Too often training sessions draw to a close with no ending exercise to bring closure. An evaluation may be completed, but there is no shared experience, no review, no checking on expectations, no saying good-bye. Blame this on a lack of time or a lack of understanding, but it is important to your learners that you close the loop. The closing of a learning session gives learners one last time to review what they learned or practice skills before returning to the workplace. The best way to make learning stick is through practice and review. Making the practice and review fun and interesting adds to the "stickiness." The activities in this section help make the learning stick.

82   Stump the Teams Review

Overview

Use this strategy to review content at the end of a learning session.

Participants

8 to 40 participants in teams of three to six

Procedure

1. After all content has been covered, divide into as many teams that make sense for the overall size of the group.

2. Allow the teams to have 5 to 10 minutes to review all material (open book), including notes taken, to come up with five to seven questions with correct answers to ask the other teams. They will use fewer questions, but this ensures that each team has enough questions if another team uses the same question.

3. Ask the teams to select a spokesperson for each team to ask the questions and answer for the team.

4. During the setup, you may want to make the rounds to ensure the teams are developing questions from the content (no trick questions).

5. One team at a time will present one question to the other teams; you will recognize the team whose spokesperson raises a hand first. That team has five seconds to answer the question. If the team answers correctly, they will present the next question. If they do not have the correct answer, the question is presented again to the rest of the teams. The asking team decides if the answer is correct. You may need to step in for any disagreements.

6. This continues until all teams have had an opportunity to ask a question.

7. Teams giving correct answers may be recognized with small rewards, even if it is points compiled on a flipchart page.

Debrief

- We have covered a great deal of information. What did this review tell you about how much you have retained?

- How will this knowledge make a difference in your everyday work habits?

- What areas do you still need to perfect? What ideas do you have to accomplish that?

Variations

1. You may want to go over the questions that were missed or the group had difficulty answering correctly.

2. For a smaller group you may want to continue for two to four rounds.

3. "Stump the Trainer" is the same premise; however, the teams ask the questions of the trainer. Participants generally display more excitement from this version. They tend to dig a little deeper for questions to stump the trainer. You may purposely miss all or a portion of a question, and ask the participants to elaborate on the answer they have.

4. Instead of waiting until the end of a session, you could use this strategy after a heavy content area, or in the afternoon as an energizer.

Case Example

In a session with new hospitality employees you may ask questions such as:

- How will what you have learned help you encourage return visits from our guests?

- We have over X number of departments. Which department would you recommend to a guest that was looking for X?

- Why would the history of our company be of any interest to our guests?

Contributed by Denis Anderson, Images by Denis J. Anderson

83 Traps and Exits

Overview

Use this strategy to prepare participants for application of a new skill in their jobs.

Participants

3 to 39 participants in a classroom or virtual setting

Procedure

1. Briefly recap what is required of participants to apply the identified skill (which has just been discussed in the workshop) in their everyday roles using flipchart, whiteboard, electronic media, or PowerPoint.

2. Individually have participants consider a real situation(s) where they could apply this skill in the next two weeks, and write those down.

3. Tell participants to think through:

   ◆ What obstacles (or traps) they may encounter due to work environment circumstances or personal style preferences that might inhibit effective application of this new skill.

   ◆ What solutions could help them get through the obstacles successfully.

4. Ask participants to meet in trios to discuss (if virtual, this requires virtual breakout rooms). The first person presents his or her anticipated trap(s) and proposed solutions (exits). Others listen, reflect what the person has shared, and provide additional tips for solutions/exits based on their own past successes. State a completion time.

5. Repeat step four so that everyone has a turn to present.

6. As groups finish, lead a large group debrief.

Debrief

- In what ways did this discussion help prepare you for application of the skill on the job?

- To what degree has this discussion increased the likelihood of applying this new skill effectively in the next week?

- What additional support will you need, back at your workplace, to make a successful application?

Variations

1. Use pairs instead of trios if time is limited. Or, use quads instead if participants would benefit from greater exposure of application examples.

2. If the workshop addresses a complex skill and there is sufficient time, have participants consider both types of traps: internal (e.g., their own style, preference, known resistance), and external (e.g., team norms, stakeholder interests, interpersonal challenges).

Case Example

In a managerial workshop on delegating a stretch developmental assignment to their employees:

- Consider an upcoming opportunity to apply this skill in order to grow your employee, and the likely circumstances surrounding that application.

- Knowing your own tendencies and preferences (and potential risks involved with this), what are potential personal obstacles which could arise for you?

- Given the surrounding work environment (demands of the clients, deadlines, past department norms for delegation) what are the most likely push-backs you will receive in delegating this stretch assignment to your employee?

- What are practical solutions for either preempting or addressing these obstacles?

Contributed by Wendy Axelrod, Talent Savvy Manager, LLC

84   Summarize It

─────── **Overview** ───────

Use this strategy to wrap up the learning event and provide a summary of key content.

Participants

Ideal with a group of 15 or more

Procedure

1. Divide the group into teams of four or five. Identify the various topic/content areas from the program and assign one topic per team. Ask each team to create a 5- to 15-minute overview (depending on the length of the program) highlighting the key learning points for their respective topic.

2. Tell participants to get creative. They can provide their overview in any fashion (e.g., flipchart presentation, Q&A, role play, skit, song, and so forth).

3. Give teams approximately 15 minutes to create the overview. More time may be needed if the presentations are longer. Encourage all team members to participate not only in creating but also presenting the summary.

4. Ask for a volunteer to begin the presentations or present in the order of the workshop content. After each presentation, acknowledge the team (e.g., clap, standing ovation).

5. When all presentations have been completed, ask participants to create an individual learning plan to apply learning to the workplace.

Debrief

- What questions do you have for this team?
- What else did you learn from this particular unit?
- What will you be able to apply immediately on the job?

Variation

In a small group, assign more than one unit/content area per team. In a large group, divide the room in half and assign each topic to two different subgroups. Each half of the room will have simultaneous presentations.

Case examples

1. In a four-day leadership development training, each team presented a review of one day's content area. The summaries reinforced key learning points and highlighted program content. The last half-day of the program was reserved for the overviews (preparation and presentation). More in-depth summaries provided opportunity for creative, active presentations.

2. In a one-day customer service training, the program objectives were identified at the beginning of the program. Each team was assigned one objective to highlight and showcase key learnings as part of the wrap-up. Presentations were short (five minutes per topic).

Contributed by Diane Hamilton, PCC, SPHR, Calibra

85   Reflection Circles

─────────────────── **Overview** ───────────────────

Reflection circles are used to help participants share new ideas and to deepen the learning experience using an efficient structure utilizing minimal with maximum results.

Participants

25 or more participants

Procedure

1. Arrange chairs in five circles so that there are five chairs in each circle. Circles are numbered 1 to 5. The following scenario is for 25 participants, but you can adjust the guidelines to meet the size of your training group.

2. Put an index card on each chair. On one side of the card, there is the number of the circle. On the other side there is one of the numbers (1 to 5). Thus, in each circle, all participants have the same number on one side and a different number on the other side. Ask the participants to join a circle of their choice.

3. Prepare four to eight reflection questions, one question per slide.

4. Ask the participants to start discussing the first question for five minutes within their circle. After the time has ended, ask a few volunteers to share something about their discussion with the whole group.

5. Ask the participants to hand their index card to the person to their right within their own circle. Then ask them to turn the card over and move to the circle whose number is shown on the card, leaving the card on the chair.

6. Repeat steps four and five with every question.

Debrief

*What will you do differently as a result of this activity?

Variation

You can adjust the procedure to meet your group size. The number of chairs in a circle and the number of circles has to be the same. If all chairs are not occupied, extra cards can be removed.

Case Example

In a seminar where a new company strategy is announced, the following questions might be used:

- What was the best or most relevant thing you learned?
- What criticism or concerns do you have about what you heard?
- How will you implement or share the ideas you learned today?
- What should we have discussed with in the seminar but did not?

Contributed by Lauri Luoto, Senior Consultant, Psycon Corp., Finland

86   A Day in 30 Minutes

Overview

This activity is used to review content/materials. It promotes group learning and quick review of content.

Participants

15 to 30 participants

Procedure

1. Group participants in pairs or small groups of three to five.

2. Direct the groups to different areas of the room.

3. Provide a flipchart and one marker per group. Ask each group to nominate a scribe.

4. Allow 15 minutes for each group to write, or visually represent, everything they remember from the previous day or current day without the use of any notes. The participants are not mandated to specific lists, bullet points, or requirements for documentation other than they be correct.

5. At the end of the 15 minutes, announce that for the next five minutes the participants are allowed to use their notes and handouts to add to or modify their flipcharts. During this time walk around and clarify or correct any errors.

6. Have participants hang their charts around the room and allow participants to view all of the charts. Allow about 10 minutes for this step.

Debrief

- What was the most listed item?
- What item surprised you the most?
- What was posted that is the most important to you?

Variations

1. In "The Science Fair" the scribe nominates a speaker to stay behind and answer questions of visiting participants as the rest of the group visits the other flipcharts.

2. In lieu of an entire day's content, assign specific topics to groups to focus on. Keep with the timings though: 15 minutes no notes, 5 minutes with notes, 10 minutes to visit other groups.

Case Examples

1. A multiday new hire orientation course. Participants will list:
- Company activities, contributions, and divisions
- Company specific policies and procedures
- Organizational chart

2. A one-day course about new client implementation. Participants will list:
- Special needs of new client
- Any specific requirements of new client

3. A multiday technical skills course. Participants will list:
- Procedures
- User interface commands
- Process requirements

Contributed by Marcus Potter, CVS Health

87 Learning Journal

Overview

Use this this variation of the "teach back" model to support those who cannot attend a group session.

Participants

Any variety or number

Procedure

1. Set up a blog area using the company intranet, LMS system, Blogger, or Word-Press. (Blog programs can be set to be private if desired.)

2. Establish the initial post in which you will:
   - Explain the purpose for the blog.
   - Explain the learning objectives.
   - Include interesting facts about the session.

3. Assign participants to as many groups as there are days in the session.
   - Alternatively, if this is a large group and the session is only a couple of days, break the group into four parts, for example:
     1. Group A: Lunch—Day One
     2. Group B: End of Day—Day One
     3. Group C: Lunch—Day Two
     4. Group D: End of Day—Day Two
   - If the group is an online group, assign each group to one online session; if this is a nine-week course, there are nine groups.

4. Instruct the groups that they are responsible for creating a blog post as a part of the "teach back" assignment. In it they can:
   - Describe the learning objectives for the day.
   - Describe the group's "ah-ha" moment(s) for the day.

- Identify what to start doing, stop doing, or continue doing.

- Write from a point of view so that someone who is not attending the session will understand the post.

5. If face-to-face, give participants a colored piece of paper or index card for them to capture blog notes throughout the day.

6. Encourage the group to post alternative resources besides text:
   - Links to resource materials
   - Pictures of the session
   - Screen shots of activities (if online course)

Debrief

- What are you discovering using this "teach back" method?

- How different are your perspectives from your teammates' about the topics covered during the day?

- How did this activity create an opportunity for deeper discussions?

Variations

1. Create breaks during the day to build the post; instead of different groups have the class brainstorm the post together and have one designated person write the post.

2. Use Facebook, G+, Yammer (or other enterprise social solution) instead of a blog to capture the day's events. Have groups create smaller postings throughout the day.

Case Examples

1. Use as part of any classroom session for any topic.

   - Safety course: Have participants blog about new safety features; take pictures of broken equipment and post; or shoot a video of correctly climbing a ladder and post.

◆ Leadership development: Identify a key leadership takeaway for the day; write leadership commitment statements; or post links to suggested leadership resources such as a Tedtalk link.

◆ Time Management: Post links to Youtube videos that describe time management techniques; post suggested prioritization ideas; or post pictures of suggested time management tools.

2. Use as a tool to inform leadership about corporate universities or other sessions. Give leadership access to the blog or site being used for their review to promote learning transparency.

Contributed by Shannon Tipton, Learning Rebels

88   Reflect, Write, Share

Overview

Use this strategy to help participants clarify their learning, reveal their unanswered questions, and apply their learning.

Participants

Any number of participants

Procedure

1. Ask participants to reflect individually on their learning.

2. Prompt their reflection by asking them to write responses to the following questions written on a flipchart, whiteboard, PowerPoint slide, or in their course material:

   ◆ One thing I learned.

   ◆ One question I have.

   ◆ How will I use my learning?

3. Ask participants to share their learning in two-person (dyads) teams.

4. If there's time, ask dyads to report their conversations.

Debrief

- What did you notice about this experience?

- What did you learn from this experience?

- What questions do you still have?

- How will you apply your learning from this experience?

Variations

1. Change the questions to reflect the topic of the class.

2. Put participants in trios.

3. Do not provide questions; just ask participants to write reflections on their learning.

Case Example

Participants often discover their learning is similar to others, and this new knowledge confirms their learning. Alternatively, they may discover their learning is different than others, and this new knowledge challenges their learning and provides new insights.

Contributed by Gary Wagenheim, Wagenheim Advisory Group, Canada

Closing Summaries and Evaluation

Ensure that you have a meaningful closure for your learning session. The success of active training is measured by how well participants transfer learning back on the job. Summaries help participants compile what they have learned and what they will take back to the job. Trainers will want a summary too by learning how participants evaluated the session. The activities in this section present ideas for how to bring it all together and to prioritize critical facts and ideas. They show how feedback can be offered about the session and provide a variety of ways to bring closure to a session.

89 Key Points

Overview

A review or summary strategy that reminds participants of the most significant learning points.

Participants

Any number in small groups of two to three

Procedure

1. Two to three participants interview each other and identify the most significant learning point from this learning session.

2. Ask them to write each learning point on an index card.

3. Collect and shuffle the cards. Distribute them to the groups of two to three learners.

4. Have the small groups prioritize the key learning points and add two more significant points.

5. Have groups report out. Duplicate learning points are fine *and* preferred since it shows several learners got the main message of the content.

Debrief

- What was surprising about the key points activity?
- How do you see yourself using what you have learned today?
- What will make implementing what you have learned either easy or difficult?
- What techniques are there for overcoming barriers to using what you have just learned?
- What are the consequences of ignoring what you have learned today?

Contributed by Jean Barbazette, The Training Clinic

- What is one "ah-ha" that you are taking away from today's session that you can implement tomorrow?

Variations

Hand out three to five index cards to each person. Ask them to print three to five key learning points, one per card. Gather them, shuffle, and distribute equally among small groups of four participants (each group will have 12 to 20 cards). Ask them to place them in three categories:

- Things that are urgent to implement (time issue)
- Things that are important to implement (critical for the long term)
- Things that will improve my processes in the long run

Note that there may be some duplication. The value is in the discussion that ensues.

Case Example

A team of interns in the contract world were learning to write a business clearance. After coaching by their supervisor, they determined that listing the key learning points on one sheet of paper and keeping it in front of them was a good reminder of where they should invest their time.

90   Think, Link, and Ink

Overview

This strategy combines a recap with brief pair work.

Participants

4 to 25 participants in any content workshop

Procedure

1. At the end of your training session, provide all participants with an index card.

2. Tell the group that they will now recap what they've learned using a strategy called "Think, Link, and Ink."

3. Say, "First let's tackle the 'Think' part. Take three minutes to reflect on what we've covered and the key learning points you want to remember. Feel free to review your handouts to help you accomplish that task."

4. After three minutes, tell participants, "Now let's take care of the 'Link' part of the procedure and combine our ideas. Take one minute to link up with a partner and share your key points. Then take one minute to hear his or her insights."

5. After two minutes of sharing, tell participants, "Let's finish up with the 'Ink' step. Take two minutes to write down on your index card the three to five most important insights from your individual reflection and your discussion with your partner."

Debrief

- Ask participants if they chose the same key points as their partners or if they identified different insights.

- Ask three to five volunteers to share their chosen learning points with the rest of the group.

Contributed by Mark Isabella, Isabella & Associates

- To help reinforce what participants have learned, encourage them to review their index cards in the days immediately following the program.

Variations

1. If you're working with a larger group and want to generate a greater number of insights in the "Link" part of the procedure, have participants form small groups of three to four.

2. During the "Ink" part of the procedure, ask participants to combine their insights onto one flip chart page.

Case Example

At the end of a training session on workplace civility, a participant completes the three-step "Think, Link, and Ink" procedure:

- Think: She looks through her handout and identifies three main points she would like to remember: 1) A definition of civility that she can share with her colleagues, 2) Details of how bullying differs from other forms of incivility, and 3) A step-by-step process for addressing incidents of incivility.

- Link: She shares these points with her partner and listens carefully to his insights. She realizes that she also wants to remember the benefits of workplace civility so that she can share them with her boss.

- Ink: She captures her four key points on her index card and resolves to review them when she returns to her office.

Note: A variation of this procedure was included in Mark Isabella's *Engagement Emergency*, a card deck published by The Thiagi Group.

91   Storyboard

_____Overview_____

This activity is used to review comprehension and application of process training. It allows for creativity and the openness of team members to share what and how they have learned a process thus far.

Participants

Any number with space for working

Procedure

1. Provide each participant flipchart paper and markers in multiple colors.

2. Instruct participants to draw nine boxes on the flip chart, like the example in figure 19.1.

3. The instructions:
   - Tell the story or a scenario using the process.
   - Words and graphics are required.
   - Creativity is never a bad thing.
   - Stick figures are appropriate.
   - The story is limited to the nine boxes; additional boxes cannot be created.
   - Use of all nine boxes is not required.

4. Allow 20 minutes for participants to create and design the storyboard.

5. Assign participants to form groups of four or five to share their storyboards.

6. Allow 20 minutes for participants to share and provide feedback.

7. The participants not sharing are the producers and must provide feedback on the story such as if a vital part of the story is missing or forgotten. Example: Where would the story of Cinderella be without the glass slipper?

Contributed by Marcus Potter, CVS Health

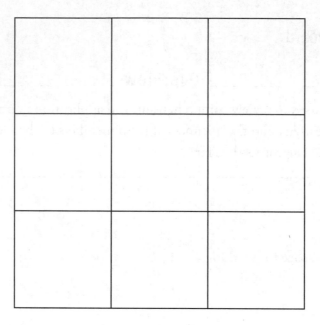

Figure 19.1

Debrief

- How did you feel as you approached this task?
- How do you feel now?
- What feedback did you receive from your "producers"?
- How will you implement what you learned from your storyboard?

Variations

1. Design teams, where participants self-designate as artist, writer, or director, then create groups with one of each. It may be necessary to allow for more time for group work.

2. Develop a game board, instead of a story; participants will create a board game or video game using the process or scenario.

3. This process can be used midway through the session instead of waiting until the end to help participants anticipate what they still need to learn.

Case Examples

Multistep process training: Story can be of steps, computer screens, or activities in the process.

Customer service training: Story can be of a good customer service scenario or a bad scenario and its resolution.

92   Picture-Perfect Ending

Overview

This concluding summary draws upon images presented throughout the session to increase the learners' retention.

Participants

This works regardless of the size of the group.

Procedure

1. Working face-to-face or online, you can bring your sessions to a conclusion with summaries that eschew bullet points and draw upon images used throughout a presentation with PowerPoint. The goal is to design a presentation with strong visual images that create a narrative flow, and conclude the presentation with a summary that repeats those images on a slide at the end of the presentation rather than having text on that slide.

2. Choose the strongest images (as few as four, no more than nine, to avoid cluttering) for your final slide that represent key points made during your presentation.

3. Arrange the images in a visually interesting way on the summary slide.

4. The final multi-slide visual summary is created through a process of deconstructing the final slide one element at a time:

   ◆ If you have five images, your first slide has the first image that represents the first point learners are meant to recall and absorb.

   ◆ The second slide has the image from the first slide plus one additional image (representing one additional key point to recall and absorb).

   ◆ This continues until you have a fifth slide (the one you originally created) with all five images.

Contributed by Paul Signorelli, Paul Signorelli & Associates

◆ When delivering this part of the presentation, you verbally recap the point
   being supported by the image so learners have a chance to absorb the point
   audibly and visually—but you are not simply reading words on a slide; the
   words and the images are seamlessly interwoven.

Debrief

If a debrief is desired/necessary, you can point out how the oral presentation and the
images on the slides worked together to help reinforce the learning process—thereby
giving the learners another tool for their own presentation toolkit while also reinforc-
ing the content covered in that specific presentation.

Variation

If you have the time and resources to prepare a video summary that is primarily visual, the PowerPoint slides could be replaced by a high-quality video/visual
summary, which is the format I first encountered before designing this low-tech
variation. (The original inspiration was the final few minutes of Jonathan Haidt's
TED talk on "Religion, evolution, and the ecstasy of self-transcendence": http://
www.ted.com/talks/jonathan_haidt_humanity_s_stairway_to_self_transcendence)

Case Example

In designing and delivering a four-part series of webinars on the topic of How to
Facilitate Online Meetings and Webinars, I ended each session with this sort of visual
summary, and then called the technique to the attention of the learners. I provided a
screenshot using the PowerPoint Slide Sorter view so they could see how the final slide
was constructed and how I had created the sequence of slides that they saw during my
presentation of their visual summary.

93   A Memorable Closing

Overview

> A dynamic, memorable closing is a key factor in helping participants internalize the information and carry it forward to action. This closing helps participants realize that action is needed to bring value to the event.

Participants

Any number in any session

Procedure

1. Ask participants to sit back and relax. Ask them to envision that they are walking along a path through the woods on a warm summer day and they come across a pond. There is a log floating on the pond with five frogs sitting on it. Three of the frogs decide to jump into the pond. How many frogs are left on the log? Take a variety of answers usually from two to none (by three frogs jumping in one direction the log will roll back in the opposite direction dumping the last two frogs into the water).

   Learning tip: If a participant answers five, ask them why? They should answer that deciding to do something and actually doing it are two different things. If no one brings this up then make the point yourself. There are five frogs left; they decided but haven't jumped yet. The same is true for today's event. You have decided to do something but nothing has happened yet. Just deciding to do something doesn't make it happen.

2. Ask participants how many know more about diet and exercise than the shape of their body may indicate. (Some may think this is a dangerous area to tread. I have been doing this closing for years and never had a negative reaction.) Many participants will raise their hands with a general laugh in the group.

   Learning tip: Advise participants that this shows that knowing something doesn't make it happen. The same is true for today's event. You have learned something new. But just knowing hasn't made anything happen.

Contributed by Kenneth Stein, EdD, CPLP, SPHR, Successful Endeavors

3. Closing action: Make this point in your own voice and wording depending on the type of event you are closing: training, motivation, teambuilding, orientation, or keynote. We have just demonstrated that deciding to do something and knowing how to do it are not the same as taking action. Now is the time to start taking action.

4. Say that they will have an opportunity to take action now to ensure that they don't just leave deciding and knowing. The action they will take is to write SMART (specific, measurable, achievable, realistic, and time-bound) objectives for their action and share them with group to generate ideas.

5. Allow about 15 minutes for participants to write SMART objectives. Have them form trios and instruct the trios to provide feedback and ideas about each other's objectives.

Debrief

- How many SMART objectives did you write?
- How did your team help you?
- What will you do tomorrow to begin to take action?

Variations

You may select other options to increase the odds that participants will take action. Here are four:

- Have participants develop an action plan.
- Have participants make a commitment to action with someone else.
- Establish an e-mail list where participants report their action progress to all.
- If you are an internal employee or plan a long relationship with participants, offer to send a surprise with reported action to you (get fun gifts from dollar store; plan it into your budget or contract if necessary).

94   An MVP Review and Commitment

─────────────────── **Overview** ───────────────────

This is a quick activity to review key points and to make a commitment to using the content.

Participants

Works for all sizes of audiences and all levels

Procedure

Create a list of the key points (topics or agenda items) covered. This should not be more than seven broad categories.

1. Walk through each point and have the participants recall key takeaways about the topic.

2. Have each person select the one Most Valuable Point (MVP) that he/she will begin to use on the job.

3. Go through the list of topics, one by one, and have people vote for their MVP by a show of hands or by standing up.

Debrief

- What patterns did you see?
- What made that particular point so important for you?
- What will you do in the next week to use this in your job?

Variations

- Vote on the most important topic of a meeting
- Vote on the most insightful comment

───────────

Contributed by Kris Taylor, Evergreen Leadership

- Have participants vote using a note card
- Have participants vote using online polling
- Have participants gather around topics and discuss ways to transfer their MVP to their job

Case Example

A three-hour workshop was held that covered these points:

1. Leading through Ambiguity
2. Leading Change
3. Circle of Influence
4. Powerful Conversations
5. Swamp Talk

As the concluding activity, the facilitator walked through the list, eliciting comments and key learning points from each. Participants were free to review their workbook and handouts. After going through the list, each participant was asked which of the five points they were most likely to use in their job. Each person had one vote (show of hand) to vote for their MVP.

95   Live Feedback

Overview

This technique obtains direct feedback from participants immediately following a training program as an alternative to the typical evaluation form and involves soliciting directly.

Participants

This activity can be used with any size group or level in the organization.

Procedure

1. This procedure is designed to be conducted immediately after you have completed a learning program. It can be utilized in a classroom setting or online soliciting this feedback live from participants.

2. At the end of the training program, explain to participants that rather than asking them to complete an evaluation form that would be anonymously submitted, you are going to ask for their live feedback directly as the last activity or exercise of the program.

3. Understandably, participants may be a bit reluctant to provide this feedback especially if never asked in this manner before. However, once someone gets this activity started, others will begin to join in as well.

4. As the facilitator, you can prompt this feedback by asking questions such as, "What was most effective tool in the program? What did you like best? What did you enjoy the most?"

5. In order to receive balanced feedback, ask for feedback on what may not have worked as well or could be done better in the next program.

6. Capture this feedback on a flipchart page or online and ensure participants that as the facilitator you will pay close attention to their feedback to improve future programs.

Contributed by Peter R. Garber, author

Debrief

End the program by thanking participants for their attention during the program and providing candid feedback as part of this technique. You may also mention or remind participants that this was provided instead of the normal paper or online evaluation form that they typically experience. It is likely that this will meet with the approval of participants.

Variation

In addition to soliciting live feedback, you could also ask participants to complete a paper or online evaluation form to increase the number of people providing feedback.

Transfer Learning Actions

Transitioning learners from "I tried it" to "I'll apply it" requires you to design follow-up activities and provide tools to both the learner and the supervisor. In order for learning to transfer, the participant must be committed to the change. In addition, the supervisor must provide the learner with support. The trainer must support the learner while in the session as well as follow up after the session. The strategies in this section can help you do that, but there are many other ways to keep the learning alive. To ensure that what was learned is not "shelved" for implementation at another time but applied immediately, you can experiment with follow-up contact from you, follow-up sharing among participants, support groups, peer participant mentors, job aids, and management support and coaching.

96   Peer Coaching Circle

_____Overview_____

Use this strategy as a follow-up, two or three weeks after the workshop, to support and help cement new behaviors.

Participants

Groupings of five to seven people; multiple peer coaching circles are created to accommodate all participants from the original workshop.

Procedure

During the workshop, participants planned which target behaviors they would practice in the weeks following the workshop. Through conversation with peers and the facilitator, participants gain new insights and energy to turn development behaviors into ongoing professional habits. Peer coaching circles meet several times, each time addressing new behaviors at monthly intervals.

The coaching circles are often conducted virtually, but can be conducted live if participants are geographically centralized.

1. Prior to the peer coaching circle, during the workshop, provide participants with a planning template to help identify which new behaviors from the workshop they will be targeting for immediate application. These are discussed and refined in pairs.

2. After the workshop and in advance of the peer coaching circle, inform participants who will be part of their peer coaching circle.

3. Participants are prepared for the peer coaching circle in two ways: first, guidelines regarding how to be an effective peer coach; and second, preparation on how to report out their experience using the behavior.

Contributed by Wendy Axelrod, Talent Savvy Manager, LLC

4. During the peer coaching circle, reiterate peer coaching roles and ask for questions before discussions begin. Be sensitive to setting up a trusting and safe atmosphere and provide ground rules around confidentiality.

5. The first volunteer is called upon to present her or his own case. Peers coach this individual, asking questions and providing insights. The facilitator adds observations.

6. The cycle is repeated one or two more times. Not everyone will get "coached" in a given meeting, but will get their turn in an upcoming meeting. Everyone benefits from the opportunity to coach their peer and to observe others' coaching methods.

7. Wrap up the meeting by offering your specific observations of the value of the points raised during coaching. You may also follow up with suggested reading or articles.

Case Example

Following a workshop on "How exceptional managers develop their people every day," six sales and marketing directors from an international company, spread over five time zones, met virtually with the facilitator to discuss what new behaviors they had applied with their staff members. In advance, preparation advice included the following:

- This will be a deeper dive, designed to provide the person being coached with new insights to get around hurdles and/or adjust the plan for better results. This gives the person and peers a chance to engage in a developmental conversation that is based on questioning, not advice.

- As the person being coached, get ready to share a "short story" of where you are with your action learning efforts, and be willing to receive insights from others. Focus on:

  - Desired outcome

  - What has been tried and worked so far

  - Complications, questions, concerns that are making this difficult

- During the first coaching circle, one director described how he prepared a targeted stretch assignment for a staff member: He had articulated what he wanted the staff member to learn, and worked with that person through the assignment and after.

- Peers asked questions and offered observations about the director's approach to handling missteps the staff member encountered. They were also impressed with his approach and said they wanted to follow his lead.

- One other director volunteered his story and was "peer coached" as well.

- During wrap-up the peer group expressed enthusiasm about meeting again, because they rarely had this opportunity to discuss their application of skills in this way.

- The facilitator followed up with one article that took the subject matter even deeper.

97   Learning Transfer Support Partners

Overview

Use this paired partner strategy to assist in learning transfer and increase application of learning. It promotes deeper relationships within a team and reinforces the concept of interdependency and accountability.

Participants

Any number of people can be paired up, preferably pairs who interact regularly and work in the same physical location.

Procedure

Near the end of a training session ask participants to partner with one other person that they work most closely with (and ideally are in the same physical location).

1. Call these partner/pairs either "support buddies" or "accountability partners" depending on your audience.

2. Ask them to sit together.

3. Ask each individual to pick one topic from the learning session that they want to focus on individually in the coming month.

4. Ask each partner to interview the other about strategies they will use to implement their chosen topic daily at work (and at home if applicable) for the next 30 days.

5. Have the partners schedule four weekly meetings with each other over the coming month.

Debrief

- When is the day and time of your first meeting?
- What topic have you chosen to focus on?

Contributed by Rob Fletcher, Quixote Consulting

- What are your strategies for daily implementation?

- How can the rest of the team help?

- How positive or negative do you feel about your chances of success at following through on your scheduled weekly meetings?

- How will the team know at the end of the month that you've been successful at daily implementation?

Variations

1. Have the team commit to devoting part of a future team meeting to having partners report on the results of their pair meetings.

2. Place meeting times on a shared team calendar to increase accountability.

3. Send reminder emails to partners prior to their first meeting.

4. Ask for success stories from partners about the number of times they met and the results of their daily "new skill" implementation.

Case Examples

In an MBTI (Myers-Briggs Type Indicator) training you could ask these questions:

- How can you use your preferred style at least once at the beginning of each day and then let your partner know that you did?

- How can you uncover the preferred style of one different person you want to influence around you each day and let your partner know that you did?

In an Influencing training you could ask these questions:

- Is there a way to use your influencing skills in a very small way each morning and then let your partner know that you did?

- Can you share one influencing success story with your partner in some way at the end of each day?

98   Creating Catchphrases

Overview

This activity is focused on creating training catchphrases that can help remind participants about the key learning points presented during a training program. These catchphrases can be helpful learning tools both during the training and afterwards.

Participants

Participants would primarily be those who design and/or present training programs. However, participants in training may also benefit by understanding the concept of training catchphrases.

Procedure

1. Explain to participants that this activity focuses on the concept of "training catchphrases."

2. Explain that a training catchphrase is a word or words that capture the essence of a training program or exercise. The catchphrase serves as a reminder of the training principle or exercise and can be used to reinforce or refocus participants about what they previously learned during the actual training program.

3. Here is an example: During a teamwork training program, one of the exercises was a game called "Win As Much as You Can" in which teams of participants would end up competing against one another rather than collaborating, resulting in an actual loss in this game. Managers who participated in this training exercise would remind employees in the weeks and months subsequent to this training that, "Hey, we are beginning to play Win as Much as You Can again in real life here!" when they felt there was a lack of collaboration. Everyone immediately would get the point and stop acting like the other department or shift was the competition and recognize that they were all on the same team.

Contributed by Peter R. Garber, author

4. Embedding training catchphrases in your training plan will help set up their existence afterward when they are needed the most. As a presenter, you can explain this concept and intentions for these catchphrases to be a continuation of the training program.

Variations

Ask participants to identify Training Catchphrases during the training and capture their ideas. It should be easy to find some catchphrases which can continue to remind participants about the concepts presented during training programs. Being a bit creative in these phrases will make them be more memorable.

99   Send It in a Postcard

Overview

> Use this strategy as a means of review and to continue the learning post-training.

Participants

Unlimited

Procedure

At the close of the training, provide each participant with a postcard.

1. Have each participant address their postcards to themselves.

2. On the other side of the postcard, have participants write down their "fab 4." The fab 4 are two key takeaways from the training plus two items they would like to implement from the training.

3. Lastly and to incorporate some fun and creativity, have the participants list their favorite Beatles song: a reference to the other fab 4.

4. Have the participants select a learning accountability partner and upon receipt of the postcard, they will contact their partner to debrief as indicated next.

5. Mail the postcards out to arrive two to four weeks after the training.

Debrief

Upon receipt of this card:

- What do you desire to share with your learning partner about your key takeaways?

- How will you ensure that this behavior change continues moving forward?

- How will this tool help to hold you accountable?

- When you hear your Beatles song, it will spark your memory of this training and your post-training commitments.

Contributed by Joni D. Goodman, CPLP, Certified Professional in Learning and Performance

Variations

1. Ensure that the employees' managers follow up on the receipt of the postcards and the debrief with their learning accountability partners.

2. Have employees put a reminder on their calendars of the interval they should expect to receive their postcards in order to prepare for the call with their learning accountability partner and manager.

Case Example

An example of key takeaways for a behavioral styles training might be:

- Notice blind spots in my core behavioral style.
- Discover the behavior styles of the three employees/customers that I interact with the most on a daily basis.
- Create an action plan to overcome behavioral style blind spots.
- Preplan for a meeting with employees/customers, where the interactions have been difficult in the past while keeping this new knowledge in mind.
- Ask for feedback on interactions with the three employees/customers identified earlier.

100   Virtual Book Club

Overview

This method is a way people can learn key concepts together, improve team dynamics, and begin an organizational culture initiative.

Participants

Anyone interested in learning by reading and reviewing with a group

Procedure

1. Choose a book on a relevant business topic such as leadership or teamwork or something a team needs to learn.

2. Assign the book as pre-reading and create a discussion forum for people to discuss. It can also be discussed in a webinar or conference call format.

3. Create a schedule for conference calls or webinars and assign responsibilities.

4. Create a discussion guide with questions for readers to review.

Case Example

Sample Study Guide

- Cite book title.

- Cite author.

- Describe any background information that may contribute to the discussion or context of the book chosen. (Why this book, why now?)

- Include reflection questions to consider before beginning or when finishing the book.

- List key questions for discussion. Provide space for thoughts.

- Create questions to help draw out how this content applies to the job.

Contributed by Renie McClay, Inspired Learning, LLC